polari plays

Published by Polari Plays, an imprint of Polari Press.

polari.com @polaripress

ISBN: 978-1-914237-16-4

First published in the UK in 2023.

Copyright © Ian Giles and Louis Rembges, 2023 under exclusive licence to Polari Press Ltd. Ian Giles and Louis Rembges have asserted their right under the Copyright, Designs and Patents Act, 1988, to be identified as authors of this work.

Cover design and typesetting by Peter Collins for Polari. Typeset in a custom typeface by Bijou Type and Roslindale by David Jonathan Ross. Printed on responsibly sourced paper using vegetable inks. Polari Press is committed to reducing its environmental impact.

Polari Press does not have any control over, or responsibility for, any third-party websites referred to in this book. All internet addresses given in this book were correct at the time of going to press. The authors and publisher regret any inconvenience caused if addresses have changed or sites have ceased to exist, but can accept no responsibility for any such changes.

All rights whatsoever in this play are strictly reserved and application for performance etc should be made before rehearsals by emailing simon@jag-london.com. All professional/amateur production enquiries should be made to them. Permission must be sought whether the title is presented for charity or gain and whether or not admission is charged. No alterations to the text or title are permitted without the authors' prior written consent. Both Polari Press and the playwrights welcome applications for amateur productions and public readings.

No part of this book may be reproduced, stored in a retrieval system, or transmitted in any form, by any means, not known or yet to be invented, including mechanical, electronic, photocopying, recording, videotaping, or otherwise, without the prior written permission of the publisher.

A catalogue record for this book is available from the British Library.

To find out more about our authors and work, visit polari.press and sign up to our newsletter.

Cover photograph shows members of the Brixton Faeries for a performance of *Mr Punch's Nuclear Family* in 1975. Clockwise from top left: John Lloyd, David Simpson, Bernie Brady, Paul Newton, Colm Clifford, Ian Townson and Alastair Kerr. © The Ian Townson Archive

ian giles &
louis rembges

on railton road

To devise and perform *On Railton Road* Ian Giles and Louis Rembges formed the Brixton Pansies, a theatre troupe of queer actors. This initiative mirrors the lively street theatre groups who were active in the 1970s; gay people used theatre to share their experiences with a wider public.

Extracts from *Mr Punch's Nuclear Family* by the Brixton Faeries are used with kind permission by its authors.

Supported by Arts Council England and Museum of the Home.
Originally developed with support of the Jerwood New Work Fund 2021.

cast and creative team

for the 2023 production at the Museum of the Home

Brixton Pansies (in order of appearance)

Clifford Dan de la Motte

Atom Jaye Hudson

Jack Nicolas Marrast-Lewis

Ned Manish Gandhi

Philip Thomas Royal

Daire Jamal Franklin

Casper Hannah van der Westhuysen

Marie Aoife Smyth

Creative Team

Created and directed by Ian Giles

Playwright Louis Rembges

Musical Arrangements Sophie Crawford

Puppet Designer Oliver James-Hymans

Costume Designer & Stage Manager Valeriya Voronkina

Set Direction & Prop Design Harry Stayt

Producer for the Museum of the Home Aurelien Enjalbert

Executive Producers Ian Giles & Louis Rembges

acknowledgements

Thanks to Sam Wightman, Roly Botha, Josh-Susan Enright, Rhys Cook, Ian Townson, Stephen Gee, John Llyod, Terry Stewart, Dirg Aaab-Richards, Malcolm Watson, Mary Evans Young, Derek Evans, Jonathan Blake, Milo Bettocchi, Ben Campkin, Gillian Murphy, Jon Opie, Lilli Geissendorfer, Harriet Cooper, Matthew Appleton, Sue & John Giles, Tom Pemberton, Phoebe Carlisle, Chloe Nelkin, Sanjit Chudha, Emma Rumford, Danielle Patten, Georgina Pead, Hatty Carman, Sam Reynolds, Rosa Abbott, Jo Lawn, Zoe Jozsa and Roxy Lee.

the brixton faeries

Established in 1974 Brixton faeries produced most of their plays in an agitprop style whilst addressing topics and events that were relevant to the gay community at the time. Their shows were performed on street corners as well as at Oval House Theatre, Battersea Arts Centre and local church halls. *Mr Punch's Nuclear Family* was inspired by the stories told in traditional Punch and Judy shows. The production depicted a society founded on patriarchal values and morals, where violence towards emancipated women and gays was justified.

Inspired by the work of other gay companies such as Gay Sweatshop, Bloolips and Hot Peaches; the Brixton Faeries developed performances that to engage with their local community. 'We believed that theatre was as good a weapon as any in the fight against the forces working to keep gay people down and out' said Ian Townson.

In a nod to the Briston Faeries, Ian Giles and Louis Rembges formed the 'Brixton Pansies', a temporary theatre troupe of actors and creative collaborators in order to tell the story of the Brixton gay squats and to celebrate their plays.

mr punch's nuclear family

On Railton Road is interspersed with scenes from *Mr Punch's Nuclear Family* by the Brixton Faeries, written and first performed in 1976. The original manuscript was handwritten.

For accessibility and formatting reasons I have typed it up as closely to the original copy as possible, including grammatical and formatting errors, character name changes, lost pages and found lines. Words followed by '/[ineligible]' are the ones I couldn't decipher, so have tried to find a similar shaped word that fits. I have not included errors or lines and directions with a strike through as they were meant to be disregarded, except for one case, which is too good to leave out.

Louis Rembges

introduction: the times they were a-changing

In ten short years from about 1971 until 1981 when Brixton was literally set ablaze during the riots, the Railton Road and Mayall Road area became the hub of unrestrained activist energy; a magnet for a thrillingly diverse collection of people who in one way or another wanted to turn the world upside down.

Nothing was going to stop us, not the local council, not the police, not the judiciary, and certainly not public opinion.

In an area blighted by Lambeth Council's redevelopment plans, hundreds of houses were left empty, with many council-owned properties deliberately vandalised to pre-empt the outcome of public enquiries that sought demolition and redevelopment.

The availability of 'free' properties made anything possible.

To the tune of 'Roll Out the Barrel', our favourite refrain became 'Bring out the jemmy, take it and open the door, bring out the jemmy that's what a jemmy is for...'

Through a fortuitous link with an expert on housing law, we learnt that squatters couldn't be evicted without a court warrant. A notice was pinned to the front door of squatted properties to that effect. We were all eternally grateful to King Richard II's Forcible Entry Act of 1381.

The Women's Centre (Women In Action) on Railton Road at the junction with the southern end of Mayall Road, became a community centre providing, amongst other things, benefits advice and a weekly squatters' meeting. The two women who lived above had a surprise visit one day from a man wanting them to look after his pet llama while he went on holiday. In those crazy times, this didn't seem a particularly odd request.

So there was this run-down area of white working-class residents living side by side with West Indian families, many of whom were the Windrush generation, and then along came a whole load of mostly young white people, many middle-class, looking to solve their housing problems.

The influx of these 'new' people evolved into ground-breaking political activism and an experiment in 'alternative living'.

Anarchist groups, men's and women's groups, squatting groups, gay liberation activists, the Gay Centre, Black Panthers, food co-op, claimants union, crèche, People's News Service, Race Today Collective and Pearl's gay shebeen, to name but a few.

In 1973, Colm, a seventeen-year-old Irish man, recently off a ferry from Ireland, turned up to an Ice Breakers Tea Party. He was so overjoyed with the experience he asked Gary, the gay man whose house it was and had never met before, do I have to leave now? When Gary shrugged and said, 'Not if you don't want to' he was rewarded with a euphoric and fulsome kiss on the lips and a chipped front tooth!

Gays started attending the squatting meetings; South London Gay Liberation met regularly in a nearby library. Garden walls and fences were knocked down between the Railton Road and Mayall Road squatted houses to create one large garden. This was 'communal living' which was about sharing, apparently; sharing houses, possessions and sometimes sexual partners.

The fortunate person whose job was well paid enough for him to purchase a new washing machine was expected to make it available to one and all and the few baths still intact in squatted houses were deemed a community facility.

One dark evening, after deliberating in a pub for a couple of hours, four of us 'liberated' an empty office on Railton Road, formerly a nursing agency and solicitors, and the Brixton Gay Centre was born. Socialising, political discussion, radicalisation, and in the basement, 'gay wrestling'; it had a profound impact on the lives of many people.

Gays in Brixton were out, and along with many straight people in the community, took to the streets and took on the institutions. They flaunted their sexuality, sometimes outrageously, with a huge element of fun... how dare people presume they were straight!

One of the lasting legacies of this time was gay political activism expressed through theatre. From 'kitchen' plays performed in squats by a handful of people to performances at fringe theatres like Oval House, Battersea Arts Centre and the

Roundhouse, a rich vein of radical performance art became a vehicle for gay liberation.

A stand out performance was 'John Vesta's Skating Spectacular', which poked fun at John Curry, GB's ice skating champion, whom we were sure was in the closet, and of course the well-known curry brand 'Vesta'. The gays could be seen practising up and down Railton and Mayall Roads, and weekly, en masse, on their roller skates, up to the local post office in Herne Hill to pick up their giros. The Spectacular was held at Fulham Town Hall but the caretaker panicked when he saw the wooden stage bending under the weight and called the cops. What followed was a hilarious scene of plodding police officers trying to evict an extremely angry and extremely camp group of gays on roller skates.

In the mid-seventies an opportunity arose for Brixton gays to regularise their housing situation. Although resisted by some as a bourgeois sell out, a handful of us researched the possibility of starting up a housing co-operative. We'd work in partnership with Solon Housing Association and apply for grants through the Housing Corporation. Our newly elected treasurer arranged a meeting with the Bank Manager and told him that our anticipated turnover was £2 million over a ten-year period. The bank manager was clearly excited. When he asked how much we wanted to deposit that day to open the account, there was a slight flicker of incredulity across his face when our treasurer offered him a £1 note.

People started coming to meetings asking to join the co-op. The next several years were concerned with endless but necessary meetings as we drew up a constitution, decided the geographical area of operation and membership criteria, negotiated with the Housing Corporation for finance, Lambeth Council for properties and ratified our relationship with Solon. The co-op, comprising eighty homes, flourishes to this day.

Mary Evans Young & Derek Evans, 2020

On Railton Road

created by Louis Rembges & Ian Giles

This play includes both fictionalised and real historic moments, and the order of time has been adjusted in some places so that we could include them in our story.

Each scene is interjected with a short scene from Mr Punch's Nuclear Family, *an original Brixton Faeries production and script, with full permission from the company. The play within a play is performed with puppets of different types and sizes.*

Characters

NED *new, naive, excited, has just found Philip (he/him)*
PHILIP *activist, found Ned. Student teacher. Handsome, occasionally arrogant. Lives in the squat (he/him)*
DAIRE *has decided they're going to die at twenty-six. Black, gender bender, ahead of their time. Lives in the squat (he/him, they/them, she/her)*
CLIFFORD *founder, stern, activist, doesn't ever bother with niceties. Lives in the squat (he/him)*
JACK *wherever Clifford goes, the mum of the group. Excellent cook. Lives in the squat (he/him)*
ATOM *on Cloud Nine, trans, never says no to a hallucinogen. Lives in the squat (they/them, she/her)*
CASPER *furious, radical. Terrified he's going to be outed as middle class. Lives in the squat (he/him)*
MARIE *activist, clued up. Muddy from her allotment (she/her)*

AN INTRUDER *doubled with a member of the cast*
HOUSING OFFICIAL *doubled with Jack*
CROYDON OFFICIAL *doubled with Atom*
BANK MANAGER *doubled with Ned*
THATCHER *doubled with Clifford*

For 'Mr Punch's Nuclear Family'
NARRATOR *doubled with Atom*
PUNCH *doubled with Daire*
JUDY *doubled with Jack*

SONNY PUNCH *doubled with Clifford*
BOYFRIEND *doubled with Casper*
POLICE OFFICER *doubled with Philip*
JUDGE *doubled with Jack and Clifford*
CLERK *doubled with Ned*
JURY *doubled with Marie*
MRS MOULD *doubled with Marie*

Setting

A large terraced house: A squat on Railton Road. All the furniture/appliances have been found on the streets across London, in some cases left as, in others restored. The objects and seating show signs of age and dirt typical of a space that is used by a number of people as communal space. Signs of life, papers, food, belongings.

Notes

Words in square brackets don't have to be spoken. Words in parenthesis are an aside, or spoken to themselves. A forward slash (/) signals the next actor to start speaking. An ellipsis is a loss for words/thought. A full stop on its own is a pause or beat. Capitalised words and the layout of the dialogue are to help with intonation but can be ignored. If there isn't a full stop at the end of a line then the next should run at speed.

This play is inspired by real events and people, specifically the queer squatters who lived in the many terraced houses on Railton Road in the 1970s, but the narrative, characters and events that take place are fictional. Parts of the script are inspired by interviews by and with members of the Brixton squatting community.

In line with history, most of the characters are white, cis men. In conjunction with the present, the casting for our characters is gender and colour blind.

Content warning

Mr Punch's Nuclear Family *was written in the 1970s and contains satiric references to the misogyny, violence and homophobia experienced by the Brixton Faeries.*

Act One

1. KITCHEN

Evening. The Squat. Doors leading into other rooms are held open by bricks or heavy rocks.

Clifford, smoking and humming is working on a banner that reads in big letters 'GAYS SUPPORT THE GRUNWICK STRIKE' at the kitchen table. Atom is painting a banner on the floor. Jack strides in.

JACK Come in come in, Hello? come on just through here through here. Kitchen,

NED *sheepishly enters with a bottle of cheap white wine (which he never has the chance to hand over, he holds it throughout) and he is holding a woolly jumper.* **JACK** *has swept up* **NED** *and is energetically giving him a tour.*

JACK *(Gestures to the one fridge)* "Kitchen".
Welcome. *(Spots Clifford spotting Ned)* Am just giving him a house tour, you don't need—

CLIFFORD *(Instant)* The Fridge. It's important—

CLIFFORD *gets up and takes over from* **JACK** *regarding the fridge.*

ATOM Alright.

NED Yeah sorry I was,

JACK Cliff I was just about to—

NED No yeah sorry. Do you know where— [Philip is?]

CLIFFORD The fridge. First it's important that you understand this, alright.

JACK gives up and joins ATOM, resuming work on the banner.

NED Ye—

CLIFFORD It is Not Just a fridge. Alright?

NED Um,

JACK It's not?

ATOM It's a fridge love. *(To Jack)* Does it need more colour? *(Holds up the banner they are making.)*

JACK Oh / *(to Atom)* Maybe

CLIFFORD It is the Heart of this house.

NED 'Cos it's communal.

CLIFFORD What?

NED I meant, yeah. I get it. My parents had a lodger when I was little.

And food... The food, in the fridge. Communal. A shared space.

CLIFFORD *(Genuinely doesn't)* I don't understand.

NED 'Cos this is a squat.

It's sharing.

Like even Whitehouse gets hungry.

Mary.

Hello I'm Ned

ATOM Hello Ned

NED And the fridge is yeah. The fridge is symbolic of this place and how you live here—

CLIFFORD No.

JACK / I like that Ned.

CLIFFORD See the plug socket? By the side. The plug's halfway out.

NED Oh. Yeah.

CLIFFORD The plug is halfway out because if you took the plug Out then it would blow the fuse In the plug—a very specific fuse that isn't easy to get hold of anymore because that is a fifteen year old plug from France—because the fuse thinks the fridge would Electrocute you if the pins of the plug are exposed. Alright?

NED But it would [electrocute you]...

CLIFFORD And if the plug were pushed all the way In then it would blow the circuit of the whole House because the fridge is a fifteen year old fridge from France and runs on a Very High voltage output—and this house is still entirely wired on a Series circuit so if one thing beyond the wall blows then *(clicks)*
Alright?

Even knocking it can set it off.

You. Don't. Touch. Or the house is fucked.

ATOM Symbolic.

PHILIP *enters. He starts making himself a cup of tea.*

.

CLIFFORD *resumes helping* **ATOM**.

.

PHILIP What are you doing here?

/ Sorry, it's just

NED Hello. I just

You go.

You said I could come back whenever,

PHILIP Yes I did.
NED And I thought I'd return your jumper,
PHILIP I thought I said to leave it for a few days.
NED I had a day off. And I was in the area
PHILIP You'd never been to Brixton two days ago.
NED I just thought. *(Hands over the jumper.)*
PHILIP Hello Ned. *(Looking at the jumper)* This is Casper's anyway,
NED Casper? But it was in Your room.

The other night was. Here *(Excitedly)*

I've never

Ever—

And.

What I'm trying to say is How could I, can I

I couldn't just go back,

JACK   The Gay Centre's just down the road. It's the knitting group tomorrow,

PHILIP *kisses* NED.

CLIFFORD *kisses* JACK.

NED   See?

PHILIP   What?

NED   It's not like this

Anywhere.

CLIFFORD   Jack let him in because he said he was a friend of yours.

PHILIP   *(Teasing)* Did he now.

CLIFFORD   That he was a comrade.

PHILIP   *(Genuine)* Did he now?

JACK   Oh leave him be. *(i.e. Clifford)* Ignore him he's babysitting the Revolution and won't let anything happen to it.

NED   I bought some wine.

And just wanted to return your jumper—

JACK   He could be a Socialist. You don't know that.

CLIFFORD   Not with clothes like that.

NED   What?

CLIFFORD They look Soft.

NED They're not—

PHILIP They Are quite lovely actually.

JACK Ah yes far too fresh to be a proper Comrade,

PHILIP *(Whispering to Ned, mock serious)* A proper socialist rejects the maternal structures of the washing basket

CLIFFORD You can't unlearn comfortable. It imbues itself / into the worldview, the politics of the individual

PHILIP 'Imbues'.

JACK I did.

PHILIP It's true. And now you can crack Jack's socks in half.

JACK And you don't seem to mind me, do you?

Clifford breathes out sternly, but lets his fingers interlock gently with Jacks. Jack pecks him on the cheek.

.

NED Because I want to be.

I want to help.

I want to be part of it,

DAIRE *enters. They are wearing large sunglasses, a scarf round their head and a long fur coat.*

DAIRE *(Greeting each person)* Hello, hello, hello.
(Seeing Ned) Alright. Hello, hello, hello.

They slam a brick down on the table.

Do you like my fucking coat.

It's polecat.

PHILIP Very nice.

DAIRE A family. Twelve of them.

They fluff up the collar.

And babies.

They continue to go around kissing everyone on the cheek.

DAIRE Or ermine. I forget. I just found it

Can you imagine.

(To Atom) I was just at the Gay Centre—we were clearing up, crape paper, it was

everywhere—

(To everyone) And I personally believe that if you let something as precious

and commanding as this—

(To Atom) The wrestling group were in, downstairs, covered in Vaseline—

(To everyone) Out of your sight for longer than five,

(To Atom) Three,

Minutes then frankly—

NED Hello—

ATOM It's Yours

DAIRE	—It's Mine!
NED	You're bleeding,
DAIRE	You're new, who are you? Daire, Hello.
PHILIP	Are you OK, Daire?
DAIRE	I'm fine
NED	How did you—
DAIRE	Doorstop collecting is a very treacherous hobby.

The boys down the road gave it to me—

NED I'm Ned—

DAIRE And I have decided that This should only be worn with nothing on underneath,

After all, fairies are just human in fur.

As they say.

They throw off the coat, but are fully clothed underneath. Adorned in badges.

(i.e. being naked) Relax, relax, I'm saving the full experience for a special occasion.

ATOM What about your badges?

DAIRE I'll pin them to the skin darling. That's what I'll do.

Come the revolution I'll walk the streets naked.

Flecked with badges and blood.

JACK *(As if it's happening tomorrow)* Ooh the revolution—

I'll be there with you love,

Just throw in some trousers and a roll neck.

NED I'll come,

DAIRE   Put it on a placard.

PHILIP   Is your head OK?

DAIRE   It's fine, 'tis but a scratch.

NED *(Meaning the brick on the table, trying to join in)* What's that?

DAIRE   Paperweight. Doorstop. Centrepiece. One of a collection—

CASPER *comes forcefully through the back door.*

CASPER   Clifford I need to talk to you.

DAIRE   Here we go.

CLIFFORD Casper.

CASPER   Can I see you privately? /

DAIRE   *(Mocking)* Privately

CLIFFORD Can it not wait till Wednesday?

CASPER   No.

CASPER *sees* PHILIP *holding his jumper. He takes it from him and puts it on.*

NED *(About Casper)* Does he live here?

PHILIP *nods and rolls his eyes at the very notion of Casper.*

CASPER   And the Gay Activists Alliance are meeting before that. So no.

CLIFFORD If it's important then it should wait for the GAA.

CASPER   No. This isn't something that can be trivialised in pretence for a party.

ATOM *(Hearing 'party')* Where?

CLIFFORD The GAA isn't pretence for anything.

CASPER   Like the GLF wasn't? It's lazy.

JACK   Without Gay Lib we wouldn't be here.

CASPER   No. We'd just be somewhere else. But maybe we'd get something done.

NED   How many of you live here?

In total?

Hello I'm Ned,

CASPER   I'll wait for you upstairs.

CASPER goes upstairs.

JACK   You can't just do whatever he wants. He isn't in charge of—

CLIFFORD At least his head's in the right place.

JACK   You were just asking him to wait.

CLIFFORD He's got the appropriate attitude.

DAIRE   Appropriate Attitude.

CLIFFORD starts to go, JACK goes to hold his arm.

JACK   Hey,

CLIFFORD exits up the stairs. JACK is clearly hurt.

DAIRE   Bundles and bundles of joy.

.

JACK   Excuse me.

JACK leaves through another door.

PHILIP *(After him)* You alright Jack?

.

DAIRE   Six.

NED   Sorry?

DAIRE   Six people live here. In answer to your question. Currently.

This is 161. Slapped on some paint and built a palace. Next door was harder, 159 was just a shell when we first came up here, but We sorted it. There's seven of them there.

It's a delicate ecosystem.

We have a toilet. They have a bath.

PHILIP No they have a toilet too. But they took the door off.

DAIRE   Colm's a radical shitter; it was only a matter of time.

But what I am saying, dear, is that these places,

PHILIP Of course there's the Gay Centre, Peter lives above there.

And we're in Mayall Road too,

DAIRE   They're ours. We're keeping them Ours.

It's one big home—People *(Ned)* come and go, but most of us here in 161 have stayed.

(To Atom) Ooh I think the Australians are coming back next month to stay for a bit,

ATOM   Ooh,

DAIRE   So you Are looking for an open room?

NED   Umm,

Maybe?

DAIRE   Anywhere else doesn't Deserve to house people like me.

(Observing Ned) Fabric softened.

Mummy and daddy won't do that here.

The council filled these toilets with concrete and set the wiring on fire

Bet your Mummy and Daddy would do that too, seeing you here.

They make these places uninhabitable, not us.

Fucking council.

(To Philip) Make sure he wipes his feet.

(To Ned, dramatically) We've got Carpets.

DAIRE *exits.*

NED   What does he mean?

I'm not bringing anything with me.

PHILIP   He's teasing. I know you're not.

NED Did he think I was moving in?

PHILIP Are you?

NED Could I?

PHILIP I don't think you'd like it very much here.

NED I would. Of course I would.

PHILIP It's a free country. So to speak.

NED What. Just like that?

PHILIP *shrugs.*

NED You don't need to ask the others
Like a meeting or a vote?

PHILIP *shrugs again.*

PHILIP There's a lot of things you'd miss. I think.

NED I won't.

PHILIP Like order . Rigidity.

NED What?

PHILIP We all spent last weekend naked. The rule was that you had to fuck someone who you hadn't fucked before. Fancy it?

NED *(Oblivious, hurt)* You don't know me, or where I'm from, at all
Not properly.
You're treating me like a child all of a sudden

PHILIP You Arrived, all of a sudden.
You don't look any older than one of my students.

NED You said I could join you. If I could. If I wanted.

PHILIP And can you?

NED I was old enough to go to The Catacombs.

To Find it. Even

PHILIP Ah yes. You looked quite lost,

NED Why won't you take me seriously?

PHILIP Because you're practically stomping your feet.

And you're very pretty.

Makes for a terrible politician.

NED I know you haven't known me long.

PHILIP Twice.

NED But how long had you known anyone else here when they arrived?

Or or how well did they know you?

I need to move out.

I need to go and Live and

Be

Revolutionary. /

.

I want to help.

I can be of use.

There are definitely things that I can do-

Definitely—

PHILIP *(Rolling his eyes)* Revolutionary.

NED —Yes. Revolutionary Yes Come on, you're not the,

You don't get to decide if I can Be

Or not.

Here. Living. Starting fresh, being part of something finally Finally

exciting—

PHILIP   Dangerous. Cold—Absolutely cold— threatened, Stalked, abused, mistrusted, Hated

NED   You don't know what I'm capable of.

What I want to—

I haven't even Tried yet.

I should be allowed to try.

You don't even let anyone Know. Outside.

Of it all you don't even

At your school.

Would You wear a badge to work?

PHILIP   You're getting distinctly less pretty.

NED and PHILIP kiss. NED gets distracted by the window.

NED   And where did he come from?

PHILIP   Who?

NED   That door. Where does it lead to?

PHILIP   Garden.

NED   He came from the garden?

PHILIP   Casper?

NED   Or another garden? From the other houses?

ATOM   *(Dreamily)* They're all connected.

Like one big space.

If all the garden walls were gone we'd never need to go out on the street

NED   Not leave?

ATOM   Why would you want to?

They're crumbling away on their own anyway.

The walls. They fall down by themselves.

DAIRE comes back in.

DAIRE   Soup.

PHILIP Sorry?

DAIRE   Broth. Jack's Vat. Is there any ambrosia left?

PHILIP Are you ok Daire? You're still bleeding

DAIRE   I'm fine

PHILIP Hang on.

PHILIP goes upstairs.

NED   Do you think there's space for me here?

DAIRE   Of course there's Space. But it just depends if there's room.

DAIRE sits on a counter. Blood is now slowly trickling down the side of their head.

DAIRE   You're a fairy, so,

It's not like you're not as fucked as the rest of us. We all heard you cooing the other night as Philip worked his magic on you—paper thin these walls. I should have you arrested. But the element of Choice is pinned on you like a scarlet letter.

NED *(Quietly)* No one knows where I'm from.

DAIRE Sweetheart I could use your pants to stuff my pillow.

PHILIP comes back in with a bowl and a small bottle of TCP. He boils the kettle.

PHILIP	Ned
NED	Yeah
PHILIP	Could I use a sock?
NED	What?
PHILIP	A sock.

.

NED   Oh,

NED removes a shoe and a sock. He hands PHILIP the sock and puts the shoe back on, slightly uncomfortably. They wait for the kettle to bottle.

DAIRE hums something.

PHILIP pours the kettle into the bowl and adds a few drops of TCP. He carefully dabs the sock in the water and waits for it to cool, before gently dabbing the wound on

DAIRE's *forehead.* DAIRE *unconsciously winces but isn't uncomfortable.*

DAIRE Ooh it's like fucking Cashmere.

PHILIP *methodically repeats the process.*

.

DAIRE My friend's skull caved in from a rock half that size.
It got all the way to the stem of her brain,
Became enveloped by soft tissue which fused solid,
And had to be cut out of her head with a hacksaw
So she could be buried.
Half the size.

.

Bit of a wet blanket if you ask me.

.

JACK comes down the stairs.

JACK Oh Daire.

He silently takes over from PHILIP.
PHILIP *moves to* NED.
JACK *cleans* DAIRE *until the bleeding stops.*

JACK This better be Ned's sock.
DAIRE It's like an angel's flannel.
JACK The rest of the laundry here is sentient.

DAIRE   With hopes and dreams of their own

　The job aspirations of our undergarments.

JACK   You can have the attic room, if you want. If you really want to live here on Railton,

NED   Oh yes. Yes. I would.

JACK   It's empty. There's a ladder on the landing

　If you want it

NED   When can I move my stuff in?

JACK   You'll have to sort it out before winter,

　There's a hole in the ceiling.

　It will snow on your bed.

PHILIP   Ned you don't have to decide / right

NED   Is this Friday too soon?

JACK   Probably yeah—Friday? No that's fine, we're actually all out then, I'm driving a van load of us up to North London to support the Grunwick strike. Come in and put your stuff wherever you like and / we'll see you when we get back,

NED   *(Keeping eyes on Philip)* Amazing, thank you,

CASPER comes crashing down the stairs, furious. Followed by CLIFFORD.

CASPER   Useless

　Fucking

　Utterly Utterly Useless

　Bunch of feckless placid Sheep

PHILIP Feckless that's a new one.

CASPER Acting as if there's nothing to fight for nothing to be Done it's as if you think that we can Achieve anything by sitting round turning houses into Homes and making things Pretty and picking up Strays and waiting for things to topple themselves

CLIFFORD Casper calm down.

CASPER But all that's happening is that they get Stronger and more Valid and more confident, You're all guilty of placidity and legitimization of a Fascist Dictatorship

DAIRE Oh really? Must have been pissed

CLIFFORD All I said was to wait and discuss it with the Wider Group—

CASPER Gay Alliance

Allied with whom, exactly

CLIFFORD We are not the IRA.

CASPER United under a common enemy.

JACK Jesus

DAIRE Oh Fuck Off Casper

CASPER And when you're stoned to a bloody pulp, skinned and crucified outside Woolies, with 'QUEER' carved into your forehead, when Another upstanding member of society sneaks in here

At three AM and up the stairs and into your Carpeted Bedrooms with a concealed erection and a Claw Hammer,

CLIFFORD You should leave and come back to the house when you're reasonable and you've calmed down.

CASPER The House, The House

In a week they take the electricity

In two they dump landfill and sewage in the garden

And then the council will claim it unfit for habitation

And you will all be ratted out of here.

JACK What do you mean in a week they're taking the electricity?

PHILIP Relax, I'll just go to the offices again.

CASPER And ask for another delay?

PHILIP Extension.

CASPER And by doing so attract more and more attention to this property. These houses.

PHILIP I'm sorry, but I'm finding it hard to believe the longevity of this accommodation is the heart of your motivation, unlike the rest of the people in this room

CASPER I'm pointing out that your efforts and intentions are flawed,

Your domesticity, *(venomous)* is passive.

CLIFFORD Casper. Enough.

Leave now.

CASPER wants to carry on, but has become too angry to say anything. He turns to go.

CASPER There is a bigger enemy out there than the damp in the Fucking walls.

CASPER walks past NED to exit. In a fluid motion he snatches the wine bottle out of NED's hand.

CLIFFORD *(Realising too late what he's about to do)* NO—

CASPER opens the fridge, throws the bottle in, and then slams the fridge door closed. A static burst, and the room is swallowed by darkness.

MR PUNCH'S NUCLEAR FAMILY • SCENE 1

NARRATOR We the Gay Community Centre present for your disturbance... Our interpretation of the musical tragedy of a nuclear family. Those of you who are familiar with the traditional "Punch & Judy" show for families will need no introduction.

This is MR PUNCH'S NUCLEAR FAMILY and to bring you up to date, Mrs Judy Punch is relaxing after her daily housework watching her favourite soap, "Coronation Street."

The Son, "Sonny" Punch, is just saying goodbye to his favourite boyfriend.

And hark! The descending footsteps of the Founder and Head of this typical nuclear home, Mr Punch.

Exit NARRATOR. Enter MR PUNCH in dressing gown/cap etc carrying chamberpot or nuclear pot. He is walking slowly - deep in profound mutterings.

MR PUNCH is passing the kitchen where JUDY PUNCH is staring puppet like at television screen with cup of tea in hand.

MR PUNCH (profound mutters) Life's not too bad these days. Pubs are plenty, darts - bit of football on the telly and the women, coor (fist up) the birds — coor bloody hell — of course there's the Mrs. If I ever catch another man lookin' at her, I'd let him have it. Mrs Punch, my breakfast ready yet? Mrs Punch hurry up.

MR PUNCH slowly moves toward the front doorway. In the background JUDY has turned toward the sound of MR PUNCH's voice and shouts:

MRS PUNCH   MALE CHAUVINIST PIG

And turns back to TV.

At the front door are the son and boyfriend who are in the act of saying goodbye to each other. They have been frozen in a puppet ballet pose from the start of Scene 1.* Upon Mr Punch's arrival and stopping and staring at them they come 'to life' and complete the act of farewell with a kiss and 'goodbye'.

Boyfriend departs.

MR PUNCH (profound expression changes to typical weedling look of a con man) Sonny have you a fiver for your old dad? (expression changes to horror and then anger as he realises the son is kissing another male person)

Son turns around to father.

SONNY No, I gave you my last fiver yesterday.
MR PUNCH Haven't got it for your own father — your own father who has done so much for you. Bloody hell. What do you do with it anyway - no girlfriend, you're never at the local, <u>and</u>, who was that poof you were just <u>mangling</u> anyway?
SONNY I met him at the gay centre last night.

MR PUNCH That queer dump on Railton Road?
SONNY It's not a dump — in fact:

((The son's song))

Whilst song is going on MR PUNCH's anger builds up.

MR PUNCH But that means you're a pervert — you're not my son
— you're a poof! A batti-man!
Where did I go wrong.

Son stops singing.

SON Would you mind stopping that, because my boyfriend is coming
back in a minute.

Son continues singing.

MR PUNCH You're NOT having a poof in my house. I'm head of our
home!

Son stops singing.

SON (Defensively) YOUR HOUSE! You haven't put a penny into it.
Mum and me pay
the rent — we buy the food. You get paid and piss it up down at
"The George".

Continues singing.

MR PUNCH is muttering aloud, working up into a frenzy.

MR PUNCH You're not having a poof in this house, I'm the head of our home.

Slams chamberpot on son's head; song is cut short. Slams chamberpot down again. Son dies on floor. Sign "BLOOD" is placed on son.

2. LIVING ROOM

PHILIP *is asleep with* **CASPER** *on a mattress . Both are semi-naked.* **DAIRE** *is in the corner drawing/painting over some pieces of paper/posters. They do this throughout, with no interest in the action. They look up as* **NED** *enters.*

NED *enters with a bag of vegetables. He only sees* **PHILIP**. **CASPER** *is under a sheet. He does an exaggerated 'Shhh' sign to* **DAIRE**. **DAIRE** *sarcastically gives him a thumbs up then continues working.*

NED *sneaks up on* **PHILIP** *and empties the vegetables over him.*

NED   Boo!
   Oh—

NED *notices that* **PHILIP** *is on the mattress with* **CASPER** *for the first time, both half-dressed and entwined. They lazily get dressed over the next few lines.*

PHILIP   Ned?

NED   Um. Oh, sorry. I,

PHILIP   Morning

NED   It's lunchtime

Hello

PHILIP   Morning

NED   I was just.

I'm chopping vegetables.

I'm going to chop vegetables.

Can I just,

My vegetables.

NED tries to collect all his vegetables over the next few lines, but some of them are in awkward places.

PHILIP   For breakfast?

NED   It's lunchtime.

For Jack. I'm helping him make his soup.

CASPER   Did you say lunchtime?

Shit.

I need to go.

Fucking hell. Like a cat's arse.

Can I have one of those?

NED   A carrot?

CASPER   Nature's toothbrush.

Thanks.

CASPER exits.

NED So you and Casper? That's—

PHILIP Ned—

PHILIP *tries to cuddle* NED *but* NED *wriggles away under the pretence of collecting the rest of the vegetables.*

NED No that's, that's fine. Do you do that a lot then?

PHILIP Does it bother you?

.

NED Yes.

PHILIP It would bother me,

To not be able to do that.

NED *(Thinking)* OK.

I just thought that we—

JACK *enters.*

JACK Ned Are You Chopping?

Why aren't you / chopping

NED Yep sorry.

PHILIP / We what?

JACK *(Slightly panicked)* We should have started prep at 157 not here—they're the one's with the massive kitchen cos 159 had the decent bathroom and 157 had [a good kitchen]. Anyway so it made sense to Smash them together—

PHILIP / Ned I never said anything about

NED I'll yes I'll

JACK Or I'll just get someone else?

NED Yep.

JACK I want it to be ready for when the 157 / 159ners come back from their meeting at the Gay Centre—

PHILIP / You and me... Being exclusive...

NED *(To Jack)* Yeah

JACK And there's some meat going in it so it'll be really good.

Casper's bought some beef that I'll / use to

PHILIP Is that what that smell is?

NED I can smell something weird actually.

JACK Can you? I've got a blocked nose. I can't smell anything.

PHILIP Yeah something smells meaty and wrong

JACK Oh. God.

Hang on.

JACK *exits.*

.

NED Are you not in school today?

PHILIP No. This new head's cut my days back. Training day today but he said not to bother coming in. I think he thinks if I'm in too much other staff members will "start turning queer".

I shouldn't have bloody told them.

A slight pause, NED *almost reaches for* PHILIP*'s hand.*

PHILIP   You Can help me with something actually.

NED   *(Too enthusiastically)* Can I?!

PHILIP   If you want.

NED   *(Reigning it in)* Yeah, what is it?

PHILIP   We need to get a newsletter printed. It's mostly written. Clifford has a typewriter. We just need it printing. Maybe your father,

NED   I'd love that. To write the next one maybe, or help It's so exciting, to be involved,

PHILIP   Everything is going to change.

NED   Yeah, I know

PHILIP   Do you? It's why usually people are a bit funny when new people come in.

NED   No one's been that funny with me. I want—

PHILIP   Everybody here knows that the world is about to change, genuinely.

Because of us. Gay Liberation. We're the change.

We're going to be responsible for one of the largest political and commercial upheavals in British history.

NED   That would be nice.

PHILIP   We're already in motion.

We're going to keep the houses on Railton Road, and then we're going to keep everywhere else.

NED I feel like I've barely seen you though, you're out all the time. Maybe a night next week,

PHILIP How's the roof?

NED In my room? Oh yeah. There's a hole in it so. But. I've decided that while I'm here it's not going to rain No. Not rain. For me. On me. In my life. Never. I've decided.

PHILIP Sweet.

NED Can I ask you a question?

PHILIP About the newsletter?

NED I wasn't going to ask [this] Or even think about [this.] At all. But seeing you with,

PHILIP The council wants to tear it all down.

NED Do you think we could try something?

PHILIP The whole road is under threat from demolition.

NED If I could, say, / for you, offer a new

PHILIP Each house, even the Gay Centre.

NED / No not offer Ask you if, sort of... Asking you out I guess

PHILIP And Icebreakers Inside the Centre—the Free Therapy, the First Therapy for people like us that exists in this city, the only people there who can listen to people from miles and miles around

NED Sort of. Asking you out properly.

PHILIP *(In own world)* And half the roads around here don't even know what's going on.

They don't know what's happening. Heteros, the boys who wait for us at night—

NED Philip, can you just, *(loud)* Stop. Talking

.

Would you be with me. Try with just me
And no one else.

PHILIP *(Gentle)* No, Ned.

NED 'Cos there's obviously a good, you know *(laughs/squirms)* between us.

PHILIP *(Pointedly)* I was thinking one of your parents might have access to a photocopier.

NED I think we're a really good... *(feebly)* Match.

PHILIP I like you, Ned. But being with just one person is never something I have been interested in.

NED But that's not, that's not what I want, With you.

PHILIP Well I can't give you what you want. It wouldn't make our relationship any Less... Less.

.

NED *(Looking away)* Yeah my dad's shop / would be able to—

JACK *(Starts off, coming in)* Rancid! Fucking! Beef! Again!

JACK enters with a bag of raw off beef. He drops it on the floor.

    Horrific. Fucking Jesus / Casper.

PHILIP   Was it Casper's turn?

JACK   I can't smell anything!

    I would have fucking cooked that!

NED   I'll really get going on the vegetables.

PHILIP   Please take that away.

JACK   And put it where exactly? It can't go in the bin—

    Outside, it'll Stink

    (I should. Just. Burn it.)

    every time—why Meat.

    Meat / that's been dead longer than

PHILIP   Just regular vegetable soup will be / fine Jack

JACK   *(Scary mum)* Regular Soup?

CLIFFORD enters.

CLIFFORD   / Any progress with the newsletter, Philip?

JACK   Fine.

JACK exits.

DAIRE   *(Jumping up, examining work)* FINISHED.

PHILIP   Yes,

CLIFFORD   You said Ned would be able to get them printed.

NED   Oh. Um,

CLIFFORD Or, if that's,

PHILIP I'd only just gotten round to asking / him.

CLIFFORD Oh. Right. Well if it's too much trouble.

NED No. No.

/ *(To Clifford)* My dad owns a—runs a—printing shop and—

(to Philip) I didn't realise you'd already discussed it I thought you'd just asked me as a favour Right Now.

DAIRE *(To work)* Perfect.

CLIFFORD / I don't see the problem here.

NED / I know I have certain Advantages,

PHILIP Ned it wasn't behind your Back Christ,

CLIFFORD Well can you or not?

NED *(Angry)* Yes! Yes that's what I'm trying to say I would have helped Straight Away.

CLIFFORD Right then.

PHILIP Come on it's not anything / like that.

DAIRE / *(To work)* Gorgeous.

NED I don't have the keys, but he leaves a spare under the,

Which isn't sensible of him at All because it's a main road but

He doesn't like to think bad of people,

no matter where they, or the area,

It's just something he's always done.

.

JACK, calmed, enters and picks up the beef.

JACK We've got a fire pit. *(Smiling, calm, creepy)* We can burn it.

PHILIP *(To Ned, trying to make friends)* The people who were here before

burnt buckets of shit—Actual shit in the garden.

They didn't have toilets so they shat in buckets and then once a week burnt it all,

The council filled up both the toilets in here with concrete.

The first people here after that lot—Wasn't it you Clifford? Used jack hammers to clear them out and got the water turned back on.

Only saved one toilet in the end.

NED *(Ignoring Philip)* Why do you always do the food, Jack?

JACK I just, I've started making my soups

Because... I like it. I've never had a kitchen this big.

.

And I've never been allowed to cook for people before.

CLIFFORD You're the best at it.

DAIRE Yeah I'm not letting Philip anywhere near my food.

PHILIP Hey—

JACK Well,

(*i.e. Ned's bag*) Carrot soup it is.

JACK *exits.* NED *exits.*

CLIFFORD Can I see the newsletter?

PHILIP I left it—

DAIRE Here it is. Finished. I made it better for you.

PHILIP What?

DAIRE Come on, you can't expect people to stop what they're doing for a block of

text—no one's going to read that.

You need to make it Pop.

PHILIP What have you done to it?

DAIRE Relax Philip, you know I'm actually good at this, look.

DAIRE *hands the newsletter drafts over. They all look at it.*

CLIFFORD This looks really good actually, Daire.

DAIRE Thank you, Clifford.

PHILIP Next time you could Ask,

CLIFFORD Can you read me the final draft of the newsletter please?

PHILIP Oh, yep. It's just

PHILIP *takes a version of the newsletter out of a paper folder. This turns into a proper speech: as if he is addressing the local council.*

OK so, title: The Redevelopment of Railton. 'Funny people, planners. They sit at their drawing boards in their offices and draw plans of ideal towns and estates. But the planners don't have to live in them. The council has decided to knock down YOUR house in YOUR community and move YOU out. We all pay rates, even unfurnished tenants and squatters. So WE pay the planners' wages. Why don't we get value for money? Why don't the planners ask us what WE want? What can we DO about it?'

He genuinely expects applause.

CLIFFORD *(Neutral)* Mm. Good. That's great.

DAIRE That's why there's this drawing of a pencil crashing through the street and bulldozing through the houses, see?

PHILIP OK, OK, yes, it looks great, thank you.

CLIFFORD And what about, on the [back].

PHILIP And then on the other side we have details of the meeting in a few Mondays and a map of the threatened roads in the borough.

CLIFFORD You need to explain Lambeth's CPO somewhere. The Compulsory Purchase Order. All the houses they want to pull down.

PHILIP / We'll label them on the map,

CLIFFORD People need to become fluent in the

terminology. It's not good enough just reeling off squatters rights to police,

DAIRE Almost poked my left tit out with that fucking homemade weapon at 45.

PHILIP The what?

DAIRE You'll have to show your puppy *(Ned)* he'll cream himself.

45 have built a huge swinging ball with metal spikes to fend people off.

I'd much rather have that here rather than just quoting Squatters Rights

PHILIP They wouldn't actually use it though? It's just for show.

DAIRE It looks very Poised.

CLIFFORD I don't see the harm in it being functional if it becomes necessary.

PHILIP Wow.

CLIFFORD It's how our actions and words need to be. Stong. How we should encourage others to speak.

DAIRE Talk like a giant mace. Got it.

CLIFFORD And intelligent confident use of correct terminology.

That is how we win.

DAIRE And with maces.

CLIFFORD Philip. Don't just call it a meeting.

Before the council can have permission to take over the

site they have to hold a public enquiry and explain and
justify their plans to a General Inspector,
Who will also rightfully hear from local organisations
and communities. It's our Only chance to contest them
legally—fairly, and on their terms.
It's about power. It's all about power.
Once they take it away from us we'll never get it back.
Twenty, thirty, forty years into the future and we still
won't have it back. People will just be piled and piled on
top of each other with less and less money around them
while a minority elite will reach untouchable heights.
If we don't act now and properly then our inaction will
have the most awful ramifications.

DAIRE / the 'most Awful Ramifications'.

CLIFFORD *(On a roll)* There will be nowhere for people to go.
New council housing estates come with overcrowding
and higher rent—at Stockwell Park the rent for a two
bedroom house is thirteen pounds a week—

(re Philip) And people like us are getting less work as it is.

PHILIP Clifford. You don't need to keep selling to us.
We're doing it with you remember,

CLIFFORD They need to be out this week. As soon as
possible. The public enquiry is at the end of the month.
And I would like to talk to you both about Casper.
To tell you about what he wants to propose at the
meeting. But to us first. As a house. He wants it to be a

unanimous front, and a joint proposal with his new... Allies.

PHILIP What is it?

CLIFFORD Just to warn you. Everyone should be of sound mind and be able to create a sensible dialogue.

NED *appears in the doorway.*

PHILIP Allies?

CLIFFORD Casper is going to propose that this coming march—

DAIRE The gay one?

CLIFFORD He told me wants to set off a bomb.

.

PHILIP You're not serious?

DAIRE Bomb? Bomb where?

CLIFFORD A bomb made here from scratch with sourced materials given to us by his friends.

PHILIP Bomb where, Clifford?

CLIFFORD WHSmiths.

PHILIP / Jesus fucking Christ.

DAIRE / Not the fucking ring binders!

CLIFFORD Just to tell you. We don't need to discuss it now.

JACK *(Off stage)* Soup's ready—

PHILIP You can't be serious? Clifford, you Can't

CLIFFORD I am neither condoning or vetoing the subject, I am just letting you know in advance because it will be an extremely passionate matter.

DAIRE Is the because of *Gay News*? Them not selling it anymore?

PHILIP What good would that do anyone? He's an anarchist, he doesn't give a shit about a real cause, he just wants chaos. It'd probably be impossible to ever hold a march ever again, if we Burned down a WH-fucking-Smiths—

DAIRE / Exploded, not burned, much more Camp

CLIFFORD As I said. This isn't for now.

PHILIP I can't believe you're even entertaining a Discussion about it.

CLIFFORD It is always important to hear what everyone has to say,

NED *(Entering properly)* Jack told me to tell you soup's ready,

DAIRE OK, I'm done for now Thank You Very Much, *(Passing Ned)* Hear that did you? You might get some excitement after all.

MR PUNCH'S NUCLEAR FAMILY • SCENE 2

MR PUNCH enters the kitchen. JUDY PUNCH comes to life.

JUDY Sonny gone off to work then? You off soon?

MR PUNCH *(Looking rather sick and evil)* Not going in today. Liver's at me.

JUDY Suppose you're going to sit there all day watching me at it until I go and do my office cleaning. Well you can get this into your head. I'm a free person now, I'm no man's slag anymore. What I earn, I'm going to keep see. You can work and feed yourself and bloody drink your own money. And another thing. My label is not Mrs Punch, see. My personal name, is Judy.

((Judy's Song)) <u>On Women's Freedom</u>

MR PUNCH *(Muttering aloud to audience)* She's not going to be any use to me anymore, is she? She won't cook for me, won't wash for me. Won't clean for me. She's got perverted too. This is a plague. I must get rid of her too.

Takes up tablecloth and strangles JUDY over the table. JUDY's song is cut short.

((Mr Punch's Song))

3. HALLWAY

All cast members are mid party. Snogging, dancing, spaced out on mattresses. Time passes and the space clears leaving only **JACK** *and* **CLIFFORD**. *Casper ends up in the*

Audience. Music throbs throughout, 1970s disco.

It's the dregs of the party now.

CASPER   Have we totally run out of wine?

CLIFFORD *holds out a bottle as* **CASPER** *walks past and takes it.*

> *(Targets an audience member)* This guy hasn't even got a glass. No please mate. I insist.

He pours a glass of wine for the audience member and doesn't leave them alone till they take it.

> Yours mate. You now own that drink. It would be weird for you if someone took it off you. Do you agree?
> Is that something you agree with?
> Can you own something that was ultimately made randomly for thousands of people, specifically, intended to be...
> Unspecifically yours.
> Yeah. Ridiculous isn't it. Glad you think so.

He takes the glass back and moves back into the centre.
JACK *and* **CLIFFORD** *are dancing.*

JACK You OK, Casper?

CLIFFORD Enjoying yourself?

CASPER *(to audience, pointing at Clifford)* I was so excited to live here I knocked out
Clifford's two front teeth when I hugged him. I jumped up so hard I knocked his
teeth out.
I didn't even realise it was a thing—this type of living. I used to write more at the start, and when it first opened—Icebreakers—in the Gay Centre they had this writing thing you could drop into and then they had this tea party style, thing. Every Sunday. And the first time I went and—it was run by / this great hetero couple actually—

JACK Leave 'em be Casper.

CASPER It was here, in Clifford's house, and after it finished I asked if I had to go. And
he said that I didn't. So I stayed. And hugged him the hardest I'd hugged anyone before.
And so my first night squatting was actually in an Emergency Dentists.
Don't you feel that?
That's what's real. That's specific. I was at home—found

home—

But at the dentist's.

That's what's real.

Don't you want to keep that?

Don't you want to fight for it? Burn for it? At all costs, fight?

Here, and all the things that come into existence with it.

South London Action Group—

ATOM *(From audience, walking through)* SLAGS!

CASPER *(Picking up a brick)* Black Panthers, Gay Press—
Because it's not safe. None of it is. The Black Panther's Bookshop got firebombed, Again,

next will be the Group, the Gay Centre got attacked,

(Pretends to lob the brick)

Again.

JACK I know, I was in it thank you.

It was only like when the police do it.

CASPER So don't you think it's worth fighting for, and keeping?

Isn't that what it's all about?

CLIFFORD Of course it is.

CASPER And? And? Are you going to actually Do anything about it?

Or just throw garden parties till it all gets better.

JACK I think so yes. Garden parties you're Always at I might add.

CASPER   I Live here.

CLIFFORD So you have a Room to go to.

JACK   *(Re arguing)* OK, not tonight thank you
    (Pulling Clifford) Come on, bed

CASPER   Fine. Go. Go.

CLIFFORD Night.

They both kiss **CASPER** *on the cheek, who shrugs them off.*
They go to leave, arm in arm.

CLIFFORD We still run that tea party on Sundays, Casper, if it's not too domestic for you.

JACK   Hello Goodbye / Night night.

DAIRE   *(With the energy of 'CUNTS')* TORIES!

CLIFFORD See you tomorrow

As **JACK** *and* **CLIFFORD** *exit they cross paths with* **DAIRE** *and* **ATOM**. *They are both in full drag and look a little worse for wear.*

ATOM   Hello Casper. *(Casual)* Would you like some acid?

DAIRE   Fucking bigots
    Fucking kicked Us out of the George
    Stupid woman

CASPER   What?

DAIRE   Attacked us. Kicked us out.

CASPER   The George?
    The George is Fine what are you talking about it's where we

Always meet. It's the black boys who attack us, / Keep attacking us, Yes it is Atom, you'd think we could be Allies—

DAIRE / It's the fucking white women thank you—

ATOM / No it's not.

DAIRE Oh do shut up, Casper. Yeah well good luck having meetings at The George now, or if you do make sure you bring tea cosies and needles and deep cover of a knitting group.

CASPER What did you do?

DAIRE No idea.

ATOM We weren't doing anything...

DAIRE / Just trying to make some friends. On some tables.

ATOM That loudly...

DAIRE And the bar.

ATOM Were we?

CASPER And she kicked you out?

DAIRE Barred!

CASPER What? But we always use The George.

DAIRE I knew something was up. The other day she made these,

Comments on my badges

CASPER *(Reading the badge)* "Down with heterosexuals?"

DAIRE Plus she's racist. She wouldn't let the Panthers in the other week.

ATOM What did you mean, 'black boys'?

CASPER The Jamaican boys. The ones who follow us home Every Night, the ones who attacked the Gay Centre, TV through the window.

Everyone around here hates us.

DAIRE A white woman with a pram spat in my face this morning.

ATOM It's not every night and it's not all of them. We have Jamaican families squatting in some of the properties in Lambeth, and helping with the food co-op. In 121, there's a black squat, I lived there for a bit when my room flooded here.

It's not all of them, and it's not all of us.

DAIRE Pearl's Shebeen, the bar on This road, Pearl's own house turned into a bar, the guys in there love fucking a white guy,

ATOM *(Reminiscing)* The Common's very diverse around 1am,

CASPER That's not what I'm saying.

DAIRE She's Jamaican and She's never thrown anyone out, Even when I bring this lot and it says 'lesbians only',

ATOM Mmm.

DAIRE The George on the other hand—I say fucking torch it come the Revolution.

Hang on Atom babe why don't we just go to Pearls?

(To self) Why didn't we just go there in the first place?

CASPER When have we ever done anything important

together though? Politically. Anything organised. They came here, they should—

ATOM The Jamaican's came to London. Casper. To Brixton. A huge established community on top of another huge established community.

And then came us. Layer upon layer upon layer.

And at the moment we're refusing to lace together.

No-one's asking Me but I think the fault lies within the bottom layer, right in the epicentre. It's region not race. Those kids are taught to hate us. When you're weaving a basket the whole thing falls apart if you don't get the base right.

All you're doing, Casper, is continuing the tradition of the white community who rejected the Jamaican community that came before us, violence begets violence, bigotry is cyclic.

CASPER So what, we should just lay down and take it?

ATOM We need to build—

CASPER Build what? Fucking baskets, float them down the Thames packed with flowers, good intention and Community Spirit.

ATOM *(Losing the thread of the argument, to Daire)*

Everything's much clearer when you're on acid isn't it.

DAIRE *(Agreeing)* Mm.

Casper darling, your voice is really annoying you know. Very grating. Whiney.

ATOM   I can't actually weave

CASPER   You have this perception of me, just because I'm rightfully angry. Just Because I stand up for myself. For us.

DAIRE   No it's not that. It's just you're no fun.

ATOM   It's 30p to have a tour round Westminster. The Cathedral.

DAIRE   Daylight robbery darling.

CASPER *(Talking to the audience member again, defensive)* I know what Good People look like!

DAIRE   Oh leave them be.

CASPER   There's a housing officer. From the council, I met him early on when he was doing the rounds of a property in a house we'd already bagged.

We got to know each other and now he let's me know whenever a house that's sitting unattended is on their chopping block.

We send people into them before they fuck up the insides, before they can do anything. So we can save it. He loves the houses.

Even though it could cost him his reputation, he doesn't want to see good houses go to waste.

I know what good people look like. I can do that I can see them.

I know it's not everyone.

But it's not enough. It will never be enough, for real change.

DAIRE   Casper, please

I know I'm one to talk—talking sense—but Clifford
spoke to us and what you're Thinking... Whatever you're
planning, whoever you're replacing our meetings with,

CASPER I'm fed up. I'm fed up of things getting worse not
better, no matter how much we try.

ATOM Oh come on, Things Are better.

CASPER I thought maybe,

You, Daire.

Have a good party.

CASPER exits.

DAIRE *(Sighs)* Fucking hell.

What say you, my gorgeous. Pearl's?

ATOM *(Dreamily)* Yeah. We should.

DAIRE Should what?

ATOM We should. In the garden. We should knock
down all the walls,

Open it up totally. All the way down the road.

Make a field, fill it will chickens and never leave,

DAIRE Yeah. Good idea. Let's go Pearl's. She'll have us

ATOM Wait, wait—

ATOM tucks some hair behind DAIRE's ear.

Thank you, comrade.

They leave.

MR PUNCH'S NUCLEAR FAMILY • SCENE 3

Punch is singing. Crash of front door as Cop enters - goes to Son's body, takes out notebook/pencil. Shakes Son. No response. Cop writes conclusion down from his investigations into his notebook. Goes into the kitchen, does likewise with Judy Punch.

Cop turns to regard Mr Punch with stern questioning air.

Punch breaks off song, turns from audience to Cop. Remarks rather stiffly:

PUNCH You might have knocked.
COP I heard a disturbance Mr Punch. It is my duty to kick the
    door down when I hear a disturbance.

Punch starts singing again.

COP Leave off your singing Mr Punch, for I've come to make you sing on the wrong
    side of your mouth (hits Mr Punch with his truncheon)
PUNCH HOWL who the devil are you? (Holding his head)
COP Don't you know me? (sticks out chest with large star on it
    saying "police") I am a policeman.
MR PUNCH I don't want a Policeman. I can arrange my own home
    without the police, thank you.
COP From my investigations (holds up notebook), it appears you

have been nasty to the other Punches in your home. It appears you have killed your <u>only</u> son (Cop points to Son's body) and that you have killed your <u>only</u> wife (points to Wife). It appears Mr Punch that you have utterly destroyed your nuclear family. Come with me.

Cop takes Punch by arm. Mr Punch is muttering:

MR PUNCH "Nuclear Family"?

Chorus sing Nuclear Family Song "What's a Nuclear Family without a Pervert"

4. BEDROOM / LIDO

This scene happens in two places, alongside each other.

PHILIP *is in his room in bed.*

A few knocks at the door.

MARIE *and* **JACK** *are by the side of Brockwell Lido at midnight. They are in speedos/cozzies.* **MARIE** *gets in,* **JACK** *follows over the following text.*

NED   Are you sleeping?
PHILIP No, Ned.

NED *pokes his head in and hangs by the doorway.*

NED   Good because it's just started raining for the first time since I moved in.

PHILIP   You were warned.

NED   How have people lived in that room before? It's crazy. I'll get ill.

PHILIP   You can come in further.

NED enters and PHILIP lifts up his blanket to let NED under.

MARIE   The deep end goes to about three metres. I like it here, just touching your
toes down. Something about swimming in the dark isn't there. The water's like a liquid black. And if you go under it's like

The moment MARIE dips under NED and PHILIP start kissing. There is a stillness, maybe a sound cue, while she is under water. When NED and PHILIP stop kissing, MARIE comes back up.

JACK   Very nice.

MARIE   Mm.

MARIE and JACK float in calm silence.

PHILIP   What's that?

NED   My notebook.

PHILIP   Uh-oh.

NED   I've decided to write a few things down—from here.

PHILIP What for?

NED Don't know yet. But it just feels good to start.

.

PHILIP Well, Do you like it here?

NED I love being able to come in at whatever time and knowing that someone is here to get together to cook a meal with.
Being able to sit around the table with five, six, seven or eight other people, clever, funny men—

PHILIP So are you going to stay?

NED Maybe. If not here, still Here. This road. I love the vibe at 157, plus they have a working bathroom—

PHILIP That's nice. *(Implying something, maybe nudging him)* Looked like you had a good night at the party,

NED *(Plays along for a moment)* Yeah I did.
Better than the Catacombs.

PHILIP Oh?

NED Yeah. The Coleherne is fine—it serves a purpose: A space for men to finally let themselves be attracted to who they want.

PHILIP It's mostly leather daddies bitching about interior design.

NED Which is fine. And when I went—I met you—and I'm grateful, but. But in this house, houses like this, everyone just seemed a lot more... open. There wasn't this,

Skirting board of shame wrapped around the room, the floor wasn't all sticky with terrified glances.

Here it is... Loud. Messy. Confrontational. Casper, Daire, And here, or the Gay Centre it isn't just a room full of men—

PHILIP Nearly every house on Railton is full of men, Ned—

NED Yeah, but, you know—this area, similar people—squatters, it's not just gay men. It's a patchwork of people. Like, all the lesbians are supposed to be in Vauxhall—

But some of them were there—And hetero people! Even.

And they were nice. Weird.

And sex was everywhere but it was also the smallest thing in the world. You know? It was there, no judgement. Free. The costumes. Makeup. Boys. Tinsel.

That guy dressed as a

lampshade on stilts—spinning—

PHILIP (*i.e. the boy Ned met at the party, changing the subject*) He looked cute.

NED What? Oh. He was. It was nice to be able to just...

PHILIP *laughs.*

NED You know, to be able to have the chance to—
PHILIP Do the walk of shame?
NED Yes!

PHILIP   Good!

NED   Good!

They start kissing again, maybe just resting in each other's arms. NED *gets lost in thought.*

JACK   Just get in!

CLIFFORD *(From off)* I need to put the ladder down

MARIE   Don't put it down yet we need it to get back over the wall when we leave

JACK   Otherwise people will see it

MARIE   There's no-one To see it, there's no one around

JACK   Just get In Clifford

CLIFFORD *(On way in)* Coming, coming

CLIFFORD *arrives at the side of the pool. He's in his pants.*

   Oh Christ it's cold

MARIE   You'll get used to it. Nice pants

CLIFFORD It's Jack's turn to wear the trunks. Wouldn't make sense to have two

MARIE   *(Teasing)* No 'course not

JACK   We share a rucksack.

   (Clifford still hesitating) It's fine once you're in properly!

CLIFFORD *jumps in. Jack was lying, it's freezing.*

.

MARIE Feels weird this

JACK What, swimming in the rain?

MARIE No no, God no, we come every Saturday night, even in the winter.

We just do it nude though.

CLIFFORD Oh

MARIE We just don't care.

JACK *(Defensive)* Well we don't care either.

CLIFFORD I just like my pants.

MARIE Well not last Saturday. We went to see Otherwise Engaged by Alan Bates, who looked youthful for thirty-nine. And quite sweet.

.

JACK You can take yours off if you want.

MARIE No no, I'll keep it on. Why not.

They float happily.

NED To—not do what straight people do because we shouldn't Want to "be able" to do what they do— we should just have the same chance to do whatever, wherever,

PHILIP To fuck it up.

NED Yeah exactly to fuck it up, that's it, what I'm trying to say. We—gay people aren't given the same chance as hetro people. The only way you learn in life is by getting it all wrong first. Relationships, work, homes, attitude, Walk.

We—*(Freezing)*

Did you just hear something?

PHILIP *(Ignoring, continuing)* No. We're not. It's happening too slow. Things aren't getting any better.

Four years ago we had our first march and started writing our own press and already it's been banned—

NED From one place. And I actually think they are getting better / that's not what I meant to—

PHILIP Things don't naturally progress for us. That's our lot, Ned. It's only a matter of time till something serious—really serious—happens to one of us. Or one of us Does something, They might have made it legal for us to fuck / for me to fuck you. but it's on their terms— the message is 'keep quiet, take the win and fade away'

NED *(Calming)* Two years ago you set up a twenty-four hour telephone support line for gays, right? And is still going. Anyone in the country can call that room, just down the road. And someone will answer. Probably Jack.

PHILIP Yeah, have you spoken to anyone who's worked on those phones? Half the time it's kids laughing, the other half it's / someone threatening to torch the place, or it's a married man from Wales Wanking—

NED It's not half, yes I Have spoken to people, and

even if it is a bunch of perverts, someone is there to
answer. Philip. Guaranteed. Until it's me or you or
anyone in this house who needs it. Listen!
Someone like Us, talking to someone openly about what
they're going through for the first time in their lives.
I think that's pretty remarkable.

PHILIP   Give it time.

NED   What?

PHILIP   You'll be just as disenfranchised as the rest of us.

NED   Hey what's happened to Miss 'We The People' 1976?

PHILIP   *(Sighs, not unhappily)* I don't know. Maybe I just like being a contrarian around you.

NED   Well that's what I'm putting down in this.

PHILIP   Me being a knob?

NED   No! Yes. All the good.
I don't know what it'll be or how accurate or necessary it will be to anyone in the future but, for me,
I just want to document life here
Because, Philip, there is more than I have ever encountered here, in my little life, and frankly, I don't know what else to do with it.

PHILIP   Ooft you sounded better talking about the revolution.

NED   I want you,
To tell me about more stuff, more details about life here,

PHILIP *makes a face.*

NED Please please please I'll suck you off,

PHILIP *laughs.*

NED Or I'll never leave this room and I'll piss and shit myself in your lovely room on your / lovely bed,
Where are you getting these sheets from?

PHILIP Ew Ned, OK, OK fine fine

PHILIP *flips* **NED** *onto his back and presses him down. They kiss.*

JACK I've not been swimming for ages. And not outside to a lido since my parents used to take me,

MARIE You should join us. Why change the world if you're not going to have fun doing it.

CLIFFORD It's so calm.

MARIE As long as you put the ladder back over that wall when you're done you can come anytime. Bring anyone. It's like bringing our little version of the world from Railton Road out into the real world for a while. We can squat anywhere we like, even Brockwell Lido,

JACK Yeah it's fucking great, I'm just not good with the cold

CLIFFORD *hugs him and rubs his shoulders vigorously.*

MARIE   It's 'cos you're doggy paddling, do some proper lengths—

MARIE laughs and swims off. She floats by herself. JACK and CLIFFORD do some lengths.

PHILIP   I came to Railton Road last summer, after I'd been fired from a school.
One of the parents got wind that her precious child was under threat of being Contaminated by a dirty homosexual. The governors voted and I was out in a month. The head was relieved.
I came to Railton Road to… I dunno, [burn out?] But Daire put me in touch with the head of English at the one I work at now. And within a week I had an interview. And the next I was back at work.
I've never felt more like I'm in a family than I have here. A fucking Fun family.

MARIE   You can see the stars tonight.

They listen and float.

PHILIP   Did you meet Jim? The other night. Hair down to his ankles. At one point he was the sole occupier of a house on the corner of Atlantic Road. One Vining Street to be precise,

NED rolls over and begins to jot things down.

NED Keep going, I want to fill this book up.

PHILIP And there's this one sound council officer who we know,

NED Casper was telling me, what was his name?

PHILIP Tony Bird. It was always going to just be a trial period. Me living over here. It was the first time I'd lived with a group of gay people, there were women here as well. Men who were very politically activated and had a totally different gay experience to mine.

NED And?

PHILIP *taps his chest.*

NED What?

PHILIP Kiss me here.

NED *pauses slightly, and then climbs back on top of* **PHILIP** *and starts lightly kisses his chest.*

> And Tony let's Jim know that they're coming round the next day—he's tried to stop it, tried everything, but nothing to be done—his seniors are convinced that if it becomes an empty site then it would attract a developer to spark a Town Centre redevelopment—Ha.

NED *(Still kissing)* Mm.

PHILIP Anyway so an Eviction Squad Team—eleven of them—come round the next day to evict Jim and start smashing.

PHILIP *pauses and* NED *looks up.* PHILIP *taps his neck.* NED *moves up and starts kissing his neck.*

PHILIP They turned up and found a barricade completely surrounding the front and blocking the windows, and a half naked Jim hanging out the top window like Rapunzel, batting his eyelashes and waving them in. They get all riled up and come back with heavy duty sledgehammers and upon Jim's encouragement and instructions, start hammering against the front door until their arms bled,

PHILIP *taps his cheek.* NED *starts kissing there.*

PHILIP Unbeknownst to them that our Jim has managed to jam a sprung mattress between the door and a tree trunk which is wedged under the ground floor window board—a tree trunk—so no matter how hard they swung it was all just quietly absorbed into the springs.

NED *(Finally stopping, and rolling over to scribble notes)* Did they ever get in?

PHILIP Aww.

NED Got what I need now sorry,

PHILIP They had to go and come back and smash through a wall from inside the house next door. They always get in.

NED You think they'll ever get in here?

PHILIP   They always get in.
NED   Hm. We'll see.
PHILIP   Got a crystal ball have you?
NED   Just regular balls I'm afraid.

PHILIP *laughs.*

NED   But they Can see the future
PHILIP   Oh yeah?
NED   Yeah just give 'em a rub, and all is yours.

They start kissing again, properly.

NED   And I've realised that you'll never be able to be with just one person.

.

PHILIP   Right.
NED   And that's fine. That's fine that you want that.
It's not your fault
PHILIP   Ned.
   NED   Yeah but. I want that. The one person. I do. Even though… I haven't had that before. But I know I want that. And I will have it some day.
Someone who's mine,
A soul mate.
And that isn't you. And that's OK.
It is.

PHILIP   Ooookay. Thank you?

NED   But I hope we'll be friends for a long, long time. Even though I'm a monogamous contradictory liberal.

PHILIP *laughs. They start kissing again.*

MARIE   You should try going under, it's wonderful. Pitch dark and soundless.

Like being back in the womb,

JACK   OK, Marie.

MARIE   Go on try it, all together

CLIFFORD   I quite like floating

A **DRUNK MAN** *holding a claw hammer enters the bedroom. He stands silently and watches them kiss for a while.*

PHILIP *rolls* **NED** *over and climbs on top of him.*

PHILIP   I wish you'd been here last summer.

NED   Why?

PHILIP   It was amazing, it was so hot—we spent all of it in the garden,

NED   Naked?

PHILIP   Various stages of nakedness... Playing Ella Fitzgerald, cider, stretching on Forever,

NED   Revolution in the air...

They kiss.

MAN *(Slurred)* What

NED *and* **PHILIP** *break apart, frozen in fear.*

> What
>
> Are you?

MARIE Come ooooon, try it!

MAN 'S

> 'S
>
> 'S

JACK Fine fine

PHILIP *stands, raising his arms and slowly moves towards him.*

PHILIP OK mate, OK

> You're in the wrong place, OK,

MARIE OK all together

MAN 'S wrong. You're fuckin'

MARIE One

PHILIP Let's just get you…

PHILIP *and the* **MAN** *are stood facing each other.*

MARIE Two

MAN *(As if about to lunge)* Wrong

MARIE THREE

NED jumps up. All cast members drop to neutral. Not frozen, still in character, but neutral, calm.

NED   SORRY. Sorry. Um.

NED directly addresses the audience for the first time.

> Sorry everyone. *(He clears his throat.)*
> I just don't want to experience this again. Can I just tell you what happened instead? Sorry, one second.

NED collects his notebook and stands in the middle of the room. He finds the right page and begins to read.

> The man lunges, and collides with Philip clumsily and he loses his hammer, knocking them both to the floor. They grapple but the man is stronger and Philip ends up on the bottom. I jump off the bed and try to get the Man off Philip, but am easily pushed away.
> And the Man starts to strangle Philip.
> I call for help three times.
> And Philip turns purple.

CLIFFORD, **JACK** and **MARIE** *move out of the pool space and into the house, casually towelling off.*

> I try to pull the Man off but can't loosen his grip, so I put my arm round his neck and pull back as hard as I can and start screaming, because Philip is losing

consciousness. One eye is bigger than the other.

There is spit round his mouth.

Little ribbons of light move up his skin.

That's when Clifford ran into the room.

CLIFFORD *(Still)* Move, Ned,

NED He stops and takes a quick second to analyse what is happening, and then runs to grab a chair from the corner of the room.

CLIFFORD Ned, MOVE

NED I dive out of the way and Clifford smashes the chair down on the Man's head.

The Man is knocked unconscious.

Like a wrestler.

It looks fake.

It would have looked funny if Philip started breathing again.

NED *closes the book and the scene resumes, but everyone stays in place.*

CLIFFORD / Call an ambulance.

NED / Oh my God.

CLIFFORD Ned, next door have a phone—

NED / He just

He just

He just

He just

CLIFFORD I'll go,

We've just got in,

(Calling) JACK

There are people downstairs, stay with him. It'll be OK,

It'll be alright.

CLIFFORD runs out. JACK and MARIE run out.

NED, alone, stares at PHILIP, motionlessly standing in the room.

NED *(Hyperventilating)* He just

He just

He just...

Just

End of Act One.

ACT TWO

MR PUNCH'S NUCLEAR FAMILY • SCENE 4

Song of Nuclear Family replaced by "Rule Britannia" - as John Bull leads in Rule Britannia and take up seats on "the bench". Jury stops singing.

CLERK Case before the court. The fiendish destruction of Mr Punch's nuclear family by Mr Punch himself.

Judges have total lack of interest (PICKING THEIR NOSES) ~~in proceedings, are either gossiping together or comparing each others nail polish.~~

CLERK Ahem! Your honerables. Mr Punch pleads "not guilty".
JUDGES Not guilty?
RULE BRIT Did he do it before or after breakfast?
CLERK Before breakfast – your honourable.
JOHN BULL This is very serious. No Englishman should exert himself before breakfast (he regards Jury, who nod in agreement)
RULE BRIT Call the policeman.

CLERK motions policeman forward to give evidence.

CLERK goes to place policeman's hand on bible for swearing in.

POLICEMAN *I'm sorry your honourables it is against my religion to swear the whole truth on the bible. It's against my religion.*

JOHN BULL *Very good (turning to Rule Brit) A religious policeman.*

RULE BRIT *(With look of admiration at policeman) Carry on with your evidence, constable.*

POLICEMAN *On the day in question- (reads so rapidly from notebook no one can comprehend. Judges are taking down notes furiously)*

RULE BRIT *Thank you constable.*

[The next section appears to be the Constable's speech from his notebook and has been placed in between the two pages as an addition, and has been cut off. It will be included in full here, as I can best interpret]

CONSTABLE *On 25th May 1975 at 10.30 I was walking my head down the corners of Railton Rd/Chaucer and approaching Shakespeare Rd. When I found an indescribable disturbance that appeared to be coming from or near the residence of Mr Punch. - I decided to inquire as to its purpose. Upon receiving no reply to my polite knock on the front door which was green and silver door knock and had been recently painted. I pressed a little more firmly and lo. the door opened and I entered in. In order to attract attention I called after Mr Punch's health "hello Mr Punch how are you". But my pathway was blocked by an immovable object. I bent down to ascertain its nature. I found* it to be a body, after questioning it, found it to be dead. The body was still in a luke warm state/[ineligible] so I concluded it to have been a recent death. Fragments of china of a china pot nature shows that the body's head had come into contact with this said pot object. I decided to advance further into the house still calling after Mr Punch's health. I found myself in a small modern kitchenette with green painted cupboards-

JUDGES Go on Constable go on on

CONSTABLE -gas cooker and modern deep freeze box/[ineligible]. I found there a person of female nature in a sitting position - a little red in the face, mouth open instead/[ineligible] of singing. I approached the said person and after close questioning found her to be another dead body.

RULE BRIT Is any of the said dead bodies present in court in order to identify?

JOHN BULL No there isn't anybody here. Continue constable.

CONSTABLE I turned

[regular pages continued]

JOHN BULL How did you destroy your nuclear family Mr Punch?

PUNCH I battered my son with the chamber pot and I choked my Mrs. with the tea towel, your Honourables.

JURY mutters disapproval.

JOHN BULL Very messy.

GREAT BRIT *(who is looking eagerly at Punch)* But why Mr
   Punch why?
PUNCH Your honourables; *(throwing his arms wide and looking
   into the sky - Jury hums)*
   (angelically) I once had a dream.

Judges impressed, look at each other and repeat:

JUDGES A DREAM
PUNCH Yes, a dream. That with my natural resources of
   tenderness, I could raise the ideal son, and with an example of
   devotion - train the ideal wife. Like when I was able to raise
   the best vegetables on my allotment. I gave up my job, your
   honourables, to give my full attention to the raising of the ideal
   nuclear family - like what they advertise on the telly. But, your
   honourables, with all my good intentions, I failed.
RULE BRIT *(to John Bull, whispered)* What a beautiful dream
JUDGES *(sympathetically)* What happened? *(Jury repeats)*
PUNCH A disease sirs, set in and perverted my young crop. My son
   was such a perfect specimen. He was the support of his doting
   father. Until one cold winter's night he was waiting for a bus
   outside the Gay Centre in Railton Rd.
JUDGES *(affirming)* We know where it is.
PUNCH Standing there in the rain and smelling the tea brewing
   and all that gay laughter.
   He was tempted, your honourables, and entered in. That was

the beginning of the end; kissing his boyfriend on <u>my</u> doorstep and spending his pocket money on him. I couldn't take anymore (Punch breaks down, court groans) I eradicated him your honour - like a diseased plant - I did him in. (cheers from the Jury)

JUDGES *And Mrs Punch?*

PUNCH *Again your honour, another victim to the self-same disease of our times. Women's liberation got to her your honourables. She threw away her bra - reading all those feminist books - calling me "male chauvinist pig" (Jury groans).*

The marriage contract said to expect obedience and loving care from her till death do us part. But instead she turned out a viper feeding at my devoted heart.

I did her in too. I screwed her neck with the tea towel.

(Cheers from the Jury)

JUDGES *Very commendable.*

Judges take it in turn to chime in with phrase.

JUDGES *You the Jury - have listened to Mr Punch's tale of family grievances done unto him // A heroic man who was inspired to grow the ideal nuclear family - the very essence of our normal society // Such societal duties must be taken into consideration when you decide your verdict // Though we must appear impartial //*

(together) We direct you <u>not</u> to fail <u>us</u>.

// Jury consider your verdict.

Jury whispers together.

JURY We consider him "NOT GUILTY"
RULE BRIT Does that mean he is innocent then?
JURY Well, your honourable, we prefer to consider him as "not guilty"
JOHN BULL That's good enough then. *(Turns to Policeman)* You two better make up then.

Punch and Policeman shake hands.

JOHN BULL In future cases, we have decided that a policeman should not enter a home where a disturbance may have/or was caused or was thought to be caused by the head of the household, normally the father. The father shall arrange and disturb his household as he sees fit.
RULE BRIT Yes, though the policeman may enter and offer support, if the head of the household, namely the father is getting the worst end of the stick.
JOHN BULL Go a free man - Mr Punch. You can hold your head high in any society.
RULE BRIT Yes, feel free to start all over again with another batch of little punches.
CLERK Court will now adjourn to "The George" - where light refreshments will be served
to Mr Punch and his friends.
ALL ON TO THE GEORGE

5. DINING ROOM

JACK is crouching over the kettle and six mugs. He takes seven tea bags out of a pot and pops them into the mugs. CLIFFORD, MARIE, CASPER and DAIRE are sitting down/ already seated.

There is a large box on the table in front of CASPER.

DAIRE Jack's made everyone a tea.

CLIFFORD Thank you Jack.

JACK My pleasure. It's with Goat's milk

Everyone goes to sip but stops.

DAIRE From the Brown Rice Brigade next door?

JACK Yes.

DAIRE sips.

DAIRE Tangy.

JACK At least I think they said it was Goat...

DAIRE Aren't next door the one's without a fridge?

Everyone is about to try the tea again but stop, and this time puts their mugs down.

CLIFFORD *(Clearing throat)* Thank you everyone for being here. Sorry. I know we're one down, but I think we should get started. Can we begin?

Everyone nods.

ATOM *comes through an open window clutching some flowers in one hand and some notes in another.*

ATOM   Sorry.

She picks up Clifford's mug. Sniffs it.

Using this?

CLIFFORD *shakes his head.*

ATOM *takes the mug away and washes it out for the flowers over the next speech.*

CLIFFORD I would like to call this meeting of 161 Railton Road between its current occupants to discuss the proposal we submit to the GAA regarding any politically motivated action taken by us on our march this year through central London, if we are to take any at all. I'm sure we all have our own suggestions.
In light of the other night's intrusion, I would like to ask of you all, as well as checking in, that we all keep clear heads, and do not let the random and violent actions of one individual in the past affect your motivations today.

CLIFFORD *opens up and speaks to the audience. This is matter of fact, not motivational.*

We are a to-scale model of this country's attitude towards gay people because we are the ones making ourselves visible. We are the ones being loud enough for anyone to hear. Strange, singular moments are concentrated down into our lives, houses like this. Although we're a last resort to some, this is the choice we make. And we must not forget that it is all for a purpose, and we will not be beaten down. When We are not safe here physically, when the firing line is our sanctuary, it is because I believe that somewhere, in the future, there are versions of us that Are.

CLIFFORD *turns back to the group. Everyone eyes the box.*

Marie has agreed to take minutes.
Casper, you can have the floor first.

By this point **ATOM** *has arranged the flowers in a mug and placed them on the table and taken her seat. She pops one in Daire's brick from the first scene, still on the table.*

CASPER *stands.*

CASPER   I hear most of you already think you know the gist of what I am going to propose.

DAIRE   No.

ATOM *shakes her head.*

JACK Yeah I'm not keen.

CASPER I knew it would go like this.

DAIRE Like what? Saying no to Bombing a shop?

CASPER Not listening.

DAIRE Well sorry if the prospect of killing people is a non-negotiable motion, Casper

CASPER Of course You're sensationalising it.

JACK A bomb.

CASPER Firebomb – with the purpose of sparking a fire, not an explosion. Similar to the ones police have thrown at us on one of their raids, our houses, trying to blaze and scare us out. I want to fight back.

And we do it the night of the march, the Night, when they're closed so no-one is inside. I propose we break in, make sure it's empty and then burn the place from the inside out. Then depending on how quickly it's closed off again, we go the next night and place piles of copies of our press— the press they refuse to sell—in their burned out windows, free for all to take and educate themselves on. We will be victims no more.

MARIE What are you actually on about?

CASPER *(Ignoring, carrying on in the same vein)* I'm tired of doing nothing new. I'm tired of these houses, making them pretty just to watch them get taken away and turned into sandpits with cranes wedged into them.

JACK Casper, we could Use this anger, but in something more Sustainable.

CASPER Sustainable?

DAIRE How much good do you genuinely believe will come out of torching somewhere? Other than give people ammunition, more reason to actually make our lives more difficult, but on a legal basis? The Festival of Light would have a field day, they'd have a literal metaphor to add to their preachings—

CASPER So you're saying they don't deserve to get attacked but we do?

DAIRE Yes. Yes that's exactly what I'm saying.
Because the basis of violence, real human violence is because there is no intelligent point to make—that the scaffolding of their arguments and prejudice have no real, logical grounding. The people who attack us do so because of fear, and fear has no reason.
I am not afraid of them, and therefore I shall not attack them.
Physically.
Would be quite nice to fuck them up mentally though.
(Back to everyone) You know the other day Sandra and Jackson from 147 went into every WHSmiths in Town and asked the checkout boy to get them a copy of every paper in the shop, even the blue ones on the top shelf, took him ages bless him, piled and rung them all up on

the till, and then they asked for the *Gay Press* and when he said they didn't stock it they said then they wouldn't be buying the other magazines then, They flounced out, flounced off, leaving a massive queue behind them. The checkout boy had to stand and rebalance the till which takes ages, it totally fucked their system.

CLIFFORD Casper, think about what you are saying, how you are acting. It has no Scale!

CASPER *starts to interject.*

MARIE *(At the box)* That better not be what I think it is.

CLIFFORD The purpose of Railton Road is not to give in but to reclaim—our houses, our families, chosen families, and our way of life. And in that way we can be in control of how we live, against whatever the ruling class believe. We aren't just a holiday, but we are definitely still a home.

Now can we get please / back to

PHILIP *and* **NED** *enter hurriedly. Apart from some bruising round his neck, he is unaffected about the incident a few nights ago.*

PHILIP Sorry I'm late, How we all doing?

NED *(Excitedly)* Have you seen them?

PHILIP *opens the box. Everyone except* **CASPER** *leans* *back.* **PHILIP** *reaches in and pulls out a bright yellow leaflet, an edit of Daire's from earlier, 'GAY IS GOOD' brandished on the back, a map of the poet's roads in between the letters. Daire's pencil bulldoze design amid information on the other.*

PHILIP About two hundred copies ready to go. Right in time for the enquiry. I was in Pearl's and met this guy who Found a photocopier in the road—literally just in the road by the station and he took it home to 121 and got it working again, and it was still full of ink. So I went round, he invited me, and he sorted us out Two hundred copies free of charge. How amazing is that? Fucking brilliant.

.

This looks tense.

MARIE I told you to not exert yourself for a while, madam.

PHILIP *winks at her, scooping leaflets onto the table for them all to see.*

DAIRE Aw look, Ned's still traumatised.

NED Quality's excellent—better than my dad's, don't tell him—I might lamppost a few of them tonight if we finish early enough,

PHILIP Have we said no to Guy Fawkes yet?

CASPER A firebomb—molotov cocktail, petrol bomb—they're used everywhere. OK, in riots, they've been used against houses on this road, definitely—

JACK Casper.

CASPER We get empty bottles, fill them with petrol or oil—alcohol even, stuff rags in the necks, soaked in kerosine,

PHILIP Ah yeah I'll just nip to Woolworths.

CASPER Wouldn't even need to break in. Not really. Just lob it through the window.

DAIRE Why are you even bringing this to us? What about your new 'friends'?

.

CASPER They've stopped replying to my letters.

DAIRE Of course they have. Casper I'm sorry but,
(A) they're not going to be at all interested in fighting for a load of fairies, we're on our own let's face it, and,
(B) You're not the right kind of socialist I'm afraid.

CASPER I just want to stand up for us. To take action. Something tangible. There is either going to be a gay revolution, or a gay massacre.

DAIRE Can we just vote on this and put it to bed?

CLIFFORD All in favour?

Only **CASPER** *puts his hand up.* **JACK** *is still standing.*

DAIRE *stands.*

DAIRE OK, now Jack and I can present via me—

CASPER *makes to leave.*

DAIRE —No we had to sit through yours, thank you,
CASPER Sorry. I can't sit here and be told to do nothing.

CASPER *leaves.*

DAIRE Via me, we suggest that during the march we present and perform, perform Many times over and over again, our show: *Mr Punch's Nuclear Family*.

JACK *plops a rough handwritten 'script' on the table.*

PHILIP You've written a show?
DAIRE The bones of, yes, and we have Casper to thank for giving us the inspiration—
the world premier should tread the boards outside the glittering and infamous old tiles of...

JACK *drumrolls.*

DAIRE WHSmiths.
PHILIP During the march?
DAIRE Yep. Middle of the day when it's busiest.
A different kind of explosion. Street Theatre.

EVERYONE *groans at the analogy.*

CLIFFORD What, exactly, is it?

DAIRE 'Tis a tale, told by an idiot, signifying nothing.

JACK Full of sound and fury.

DAIRE Very nice.

JACK Thank you, It can grow and change and we can do it schools and halls and churches and streets and anywhere else that doesn't want us.

MARIE What's the story?

JACK *(Brandishing a puppet)* Mr Punch's Nuclear Family,

DAIRE Look they're all fucking at it, our wonderful comrades treading the Boards: Look at Bloolips and their cabaret, and Hormone Imbalance, one of the lesbian groups, The Gay Sweatshop, Eric Presland's productions on Hampstead Heath...
And that's just Some of them, they're Known, they get in the Press. The hetero press.

JACK Oppression that they can understand: a straight man being arrested. I've already shown it to some people at the Centre. And they like it. It could go on for years—

it has the potential to transcend us.

CLIFFORD Do you have a name?

DAIRE Pansies. Brixton Pansies. Taking something back.

.

Well?

CLIFFORD I like it. Organised.

PHILIP / I love it.

NED / Could anyone join?

DAIRE Ned dear, you don't have a choice.

CLIFFORD So, to be clear, you're proposing we start a troupe? And having rehearsals and a plan, and sticking to them, And putting on a show?

DAIRE Yep. In time for Pride. Outside WHSmiths. And for the inquiry. For Mr General Inspector. Do it outside the town hall, draw in a crowd, get em going. And you watch, Casper'll be over it like a bag of carrots.

DAIRE sits.

PHILIP I have to say I do prefer that over petrol bombing a load of staplers.

CLIFFORD OK. All in favour of Daire and Jack's play?

EVERYONE raises their hand.

CLIFFORD OK, that's settled then, two majorities—

ATOM Can I speak now?

.

CLIFFORD Of course. Go ahead, Atom.

ATOM stands. She nervously clears her throat, and starts to read from her notes. This is not to be read slowly, but excitedly, maybe tripping over herself. There is an element of a child reading out something to the rest of the class.

ATOM I would like to propose, that we knock down all the garden walls.
I would like the garden walls of Railton Road to be knocked down by us,
For us and anyone who needs it to be done, before it is done by unthinking machines who operate only for greed and hatred.
Instead of separate gardens, we would have a shared space between all occupants here on this road, turning it into a new house for us all to live in and grow.
To stay and become cold, only to get warm again,
To shelter from rain and snow,
To bask and bathe in the sun.
To share food and stories.
To plant flowers and new ideas with roots strong enough to stay long after we are gone.
To nurse, and to be nursed in return.
So that anyone can see, from inside or from above, if Aliens.
Aliens flew by and looked down, at us, at this road,
Aliens and straight people of the future and the sky can see that on Railton Road at least,
we made a utopia.

Slowly **EVERYONE** *raises their hand.*

MR PUNCH'S NUCLEAR FAMILY • SCENE 5

CELEBRATION AT "THE GEORGE"

Mr Punch and court enter singing last strains of Rule Britannia.

The publican - Mrs Mould is behind the bar.

Mrs Mould with toothy/mouldy grin sets up 5 pints on the bar.

ALL Cheers Mrs Mould

RULE BRIT Up yer kilt deer (hee hee)

MRS MOULD Should be cheers to good old Mr Punch here. You've beat those perverts down, Mr Punch.

ALL Cheers to Mr Punch and down with liberating ponces.

MRS MOULD I never let them in now. Give them an inch and they take a mile. One had the cheek to jump up and dance along the bar with no knickers on mind you...

POLICEMAN That beats the Vauxhall.

MRS MOULD (Continues) ...knocking everyone's beer over and we had women in here too.

ALL Downright disgusting. Castrate him. Electric shock etc etc...

MRS MOULD I wouldn't mind if they were practising homosexuals and be discreet about it. But there's no stopping them - They're getting so brazen they throw it in decent people's faces now.

ALL Bloody disgusting.

MRS MOULD I've stopped feeling sorry for them - I won't let them drink in here now.

MR PUNCH *Good on yer, Mrs Mould. I'm going to name my next little Punch after you - if it's a girl of course. (All laugh) Have a pint on me, dear. (Searches in pocket, can't find any money) Oh, I've left my money behind.*

MRS MOULD *Don't worry dear Mr Punch - it's drinks on the house. Down yer glasses everyone.*

ALL *(To each other) She's a good sort is Mrs Mould.*

As glasses are drained and rushed to bar. All stop in puppet pose as angelic/weird music is heard - The Gay Ghosties have arrived - led by Son and Judy.

GHOSTIES *Mrs Mould did you mean us too dear.*
  We're your old regulars.
  Remember our shillings rattling in the till.

((Gay Ghosties Song))

Gay Ghosties weave in among them with flashing banners.
Drinkers are hypnotised into puppets.
Gay Ghosties chorus line-up.

Finale

NARRATOR *So ends our "Punch & Judy" show.*
  The Gay Community Centre has amended the traditional play to provide a "happy Ending" which I'm sure that you will find interesting.

6. EXIT

The CAST *clear up the puppets and set into suitcases. They all stay on stage.*

CASPER *and* NED, *each holding a suitcase bump into each other in the middle.* CASPER *is leaving,* NED *is moving into his room.*

NED That you off then? Happy birthday by the way. Philip mentioned it this morning.

CASPER I used to think I'd die at 26.

NED Right.

CASPER Decided when I was nine. Not in a dramatic way. Just never planned anything past it. And you're... You're doing alright?

NED Jack says he's one of the guys who hangs outside the Gay Centre sometimes, looking like he wants to come in.

CASPER It's the ones that want to come in but can't let themselves that you have to watch.

NED Jack says those are the ones we stay open for.

CASPER Well, there's nothing worse than a self hating gay.

.

NED *(At his suitcase)* Another meeting?

CASPER The ballet, actually.

NED Oh.

CASPER I'm meeting my parents at Saddler's Wells at half past, then I'll get a taxi with them back to Hampstead for a few months.

NED tries to hide his surprise. CASPER smiles and goes to leave.

NED Is that one of Daire's badges? What does it say?

CASPER examines the badge he's wearing.

CASPER 'How dare you presume I'm heterosexual.'

They both grin. CASPER leaves.
The house dissolves into the garden.

6.5 GARDEN

Each of the officials Marie talks to could be one of the masks/puppets used in Mr Punch's Nuclear Family. *The Judge for the Official, Mr Punch for the Bank Manager, Mrs Punch for the Croydon Official, Landlady for Thatcher etc. Marie carries a watering can throughout.*

MARIE *(To audience)* Hello I'm Marie
   (To Official) Hello I'm Marie
   (To audience) I've gone to Lambeth Housing
   (To Official) Is this Lambeth housing?
   Am I in the right place?

OFFICIAL Yes you are. Can I help you

MARIE Yeah I'm looking / to

OFFICIAL Are you on your own?

MARIE No / I'm

OFFICIAL How can we help you?

MARIE I'm from Railton / Road.

OFFICIAL Railton Road Brixton?

MARIE Yeah I'm here because I'm / interested

OFFICIAL Are you on your own?

MARIE No I just said I'm / with

OFFICIAL Are you representing an official Housing Association or Housing Co-Op?

MARIE I'm representing the tenants of Railton Road

OFFICIAL Squatters?

MARIE Yes.

We've been looking after those houses. We've been protecting them, it's because of us that those houses are still Standing

OFFICIAL We don't sell to squatters.

MARIE Right.

OFFICIAL *(Turning around)* We only sell to Registered Housing Associations or Housing Co-Operatives.

MARIE Excuse me will you at least look at me.

OFFICIAL Go away.

We're turning our back now. *(Turns their back.)*

MARIE Excuse—

OFFICIAL This is us turning our back on you and not turning around as you are not an official Housing Co-Op.

MARIE What year is it?

OFFICIAL It's 1979.

MARIE *(To audience)* It's 1979.

OFFICIAL *(Back still turned.)* And we don't deal with individuals who aren't an official Housing Co-Op, I don't know what you think this is, we just don't deal with you type of people...

MARIE *(To audience)* And they're not listening to me because I'm not a representative for a Housing Co-Operative.
(To Official, sweetly) One second
(To audience) So we went away and we had a meeting and, Squatters Rights got us so far, but it became clear that in the changing tides the longevity of our accommodation relied on us moving our status into something recognisable to the new government and housing officials. One second.
(To Croydon Official) Hello is this Croydon Housing Corporation?

CROYDON OFFICIAL *(Serene)* Yes.

MARIE We would like to register the first ever Brixton Housing Co-Operative.
Please.

CROYDON OFFICIAL No problem at all.

MARIE *(To official, sweetly)* Hello again

OFFICIAL We do Not sell to—

MARIE We are Brixton Housing Co-Op.

OFFICIAL Well. Then.

An Official—recognised—Housing Co-Op would be considered in the selling of the properties you're inquiring about. For £3,000 each.

MARIE Right. *(Turns around)*

Excuse me Croydon Housing Corporation?

CROYDON OFFICIAL Yes.

MARIE Marie again. We've just formed a housing Co-Op with you as group tenants on Railton Road in Brixton,

CROYDON OFFICIAL I remember!

MARIE And we'd like to acquire and protect some property – property that we've been squatting in and wanted to buy from the council for some time now. How do we do this.

CROYDON OFFICIAL Sounds like you'll ultimately qualify and use our 'Solon' scheme, as part of secondary association.

MARIE *(Half explaining to the audience)* Essentially a Money To Buy, Money to Refurbish scheme? You'll give us money to purchase and then to take care of them?

CROYDON OFFICIAL Exactly. That's what 'Solon' specialises in. They have the skills, the architects, the quantity surveyors. They will then go out and look for builders to do the job too.

MARIE And on top of that giving us the all the money we need?

CROYDON OFFICIAL Yes. A brilliant scheme we're proud to champion.

THATCHER *(From the back, over the audience)* Not for long!

MARIE *(To audience)* Thatcher.

THATCHER *cackles maniacally.*

CROYDON OFFICIAL Ah yes. For now.

MARIE Thank you. *(Turning back to official)* *(Takes breath, quick delivery)* Excuse me. I'm Marie and I'm here representing the first official Housing Co-Op—which consists of a committee of squatters from Lambeth—for five properties on Railton Road. Aided by the Croydon Housing Corporation, I would like to purchase them at your standing price of three thousand pounds each. We would like to develop and refurbish them, and protect them long into the future.
Could you show me your front now, please?

The **OFFICIAL** *turns around.*

OFFICIAL We require an initial bank account for the Co-Op on file while we process your application

MARIE No problem.
(To Bank Manager) Hello Mr Bank Manager

BANK MANAGER *(Excited)* Hello!

MARIE *(To audience)* Our treasurer had a meeting with a bank manager to open the account and told him all about housing co-ops, and our anticipated turnover was two million pounds over a ten year period. The bank manager was clearly excited.

BANK MANAGER I'm so excited!

And how much do you want to deposit in the account to start it off? Shall we say...

MARIE There was a slight flicker in his face as our treasurer reached into his pocket, pulled out a single note and said,

Well here's the first one pound

BANK MANAGER *(Sad)* Oh.

MARIE Back in 1979 with our new bank account full to the brim with one pound, we as representatives for Brixton's first housing Co-Op, securing all properties we fought for with official legal ownership status.

We suddenly weren't squatters anymore.

And there was something quite sad about that.

But the prospect of a secure home outweighed fears of selling out in the end.

(To official) Pleasure doing business with you.

.

And this wasn't just on Railton Road, not just the gay squats.

MARIE *takes her watering can to the garden, and starts*

tending to some plants. All characters slowly come into the garden, and start tending to their own patches.

Chaucer, Spenser (my road), Shakespeare, Milton. All the Poets Roads.
But mainly. These houses, here, Railton Road. It was always stated that they would always be occupied by gays and lesbians. Added as a sort of appendage to the charter when it was brought up in meetings as to why the gays got to have their own gorgeous communal space.
(It helps when you've got lots of gays on the committee.)
They got to keep the garden.
There was a banana tree, there. But we've moved it onto the south side. More sun.
Used to lend my bath out a lot. To gay men. Weirdly, as heavily used as it was, not much bathing occured.
I suppose I'm not a proper gardener. Not like over there, 159—much more hands on. They've started an allotment. *(Waves.)*
The garden's a big rectangle, almost a square really, see?
I didn't have time for gardening. We used to be heavily involved in the local scene— we used to put up notices saying 'Homes Available, Children Welcome' so, you know, we generated a lot of enthusiasm—ideas of possibilities, and at the same time we were involved with not only the local stuff like the Gay Centre,

although it sadly closed after only two years (the police shut that down, shock horror) but on a national level too. We occupied Centre Point for example, Squatters up and down the country, London Squatters Movement, that was another thing we were involved with; so there were lots of possibilities to Change The World. And um. We really did think that we were changing the, that we Could change the world. Anything was possible. We wanted to go swimming?

We get a ladder and every Saturday night we went swimming.

I'm happy here now though. A garden is a world of its own to change. Our own little village.

Them over there did all this crazy paving. *(Moves along a trail as she goes.)*

(Re each stone) That's theirs *(points to a house)* over there—this one's sixty years for Nigel's birthday, but that was in… two thousand six, yeah six. 'Cos he's seventy-three now.

There's Acre there, which was one of their *(points to another house)* dogs.

They all commemorate different things.

As **MARIE** *walks past them, she can half hear/see what they're saying.*

CLIFFORD Here's the. Yeah this is the.

ATOM This is the twisted Hazel...

CLIFFORD Pretty twisty isn't it,

ATOM It's got a few catkins...

CLIFFORD (Tiny flowers)

ATOM And somewhere... here. That crimson. Little tongue.

CLIFFORD That's basically the flower and that will, they will send their dust

ATOM And get the nuts. Plant sex.

This is a magnolia that I planted. Starting to bud.

Planted in about eighty... Oh no, six, eighty-seven.

ATOM *and* CLIFFORD *carry on tending to the plants.*

MARIE *(Moving on, pointing)* And then you've got the fish, they're all of ours really.

JACK *and* NED *walk over.*

JACK Alright!

MARIE Oh here we go,

They all hug.

NED Want some cider?

JACK Or I've got cake.

MARIE Not seen you two for a while

JACK I've been around, just busy.

MARIE *(To audience)* We had a meeting and it was elected by Us, the Brixton Co-Op that all the houses on this road to become individual units, rather than shared housing like it was when we were squatting.

NED Maybe domesticity wasn't such a far cry after all, I don't blame you.

JACK Yeah. It's definitely what I wanted.

NED We'd earned it, you, the people who'd poured everything into these properties over the years absolutely deserved to live in them however we wanted. But I was still one of the newest to squatting—I wanted to keep fighting.

JACK Came back in the end though didn't you.

NED That massive bath? Course I did.
(To Marie) Sorry I've not been back much to help with the garden.

MARIE No worries.

JACK How's Cliff's tree doing?

MARIE Good. Catkins are coming through. Flowers are coming.

You live here now, don't you?

JACK Yep. How could I not? We fought so hard, and we won. Someone had to reap the rewards.

These have been the best days of my life, living and fighting here. That house.

Love of my life, after Cliff.

I couldn't live anywhere else. I haven't, actually.
Well,

NED When we brought the surveyors in. They had to move us out for a year while they ripped out the back of the houses / and started from scratch. They discovered all the bricks had worn down to dust, it was a wonder it was still standing. We saved the land, but not the buildings.

MARIE Oh yeah—

JACK They kept the facade of the front though. I'm so glad they did that. From the front, looking at it, it could be any point in our lives.

CASPER *(From across the garden, frustrated)* It's on the verge of snapping—

MARIE *(To Jack)* Sorry, one sec, *(going over)* Just leave it, it's grown like that

JACK and NED settle down with their picnic.

CASPER I'm afraid it'll blow down.

PHILIP You'll just have to leave it and hope for the best I reckon Casp,

CASPER *(Surveying the garden)* I'm a big fan of curves.

MARIE Yeah it's more of a big... Rectangle square here isn't it.

PHILIP Big though.

MARIE Yeah.

PHILIP How have you been?

MARIE   Oh you know. Married Dez didn't I.

We own a property now.

PHILIP   Bloody hell.

MARIE   I know, filthy capitalists. How are you Casper?

CASPER   I'm good. After I left Railton Road I had to move home again,

They found out I wasn't actually at university so stopped sending me money every month.

MARIE   I wondered where you all used to get it from

CASPER   I think it was just me in that house who wasn't signed on.

Didn't tell anyone that of course, obviously.

MARIE   Same school Philip?

PHILIP   Yep. Head of English now. I've got some of Daire's old badges framed in the corridors.

CASPER   We've got dogs.

Fucking hell. Look at us, houses and dogs and the downfall of capitalism.

Have you seen Daire recently?

MARIE   No. Not for a while now. We had that amazing summer though,

PHILIP *and* **CASPER**   '85.

MARIE   I heard Daire got sick.

PHILIP   Yeah after Atom died I saw them, but they weren't at Clifford's funeral.

They look toward **ATOM** *and* **CLIFFORD** *gardening away for a moment.*

MARIE   I think they're still with us though, aren't they?
PHILIP Yeah, last I'd heard.

They go back to tending the rotten tree.

MARIE *spots* **DAIRE** *on the other side of the garden.*

MARIE   Oi,

DAIRE *looks up and waves. They're in their fur.*

MARIE   Hello you,

They have a massive hug.

DAIRE   Have you heard? It's true I'm afraid.
MARIE   Oh Daire.

.

DAIRE   Yes. I've been diagnosed with a mortgage.
MARIE   You poor thing. How have you been coping?
DAIRE   Oh with a standard account, had to pay off all my debit cards.
I guess that was the good thing about having no trust in the banking system until my mid thirties— my credit score is Fantastic.
MARIE   Where is it?

DAIRE Nearby. I wanted something on the poets roads or something but ended up finding a nice flat further up near Brockwell Park. It's nice.

I couldn't keep away from this place for too long

MARIE Yeah I heard you'd gone for a bit.

DAIRE After the second uprisings, the big ones.

I left because of the police.

(Gets out fags) Want one?

They both have a fag.

DAIRE People can only be pushed so far, and back then suddenly, 1981, there seemed to be a lot of push. I don't mean just for us even, for everyone who isn't Them. Big white boys in shiny shoes in dark wooden halls. Bellend hats and detachable cocks so they can fuck you at arms length.

They reported the "riots", that they happened, but they didn't report about Operation Swamp that summer, which sparked them. One Thousand stop and searches in six days. I went away in eighty five, after the Cherry Groce shooting—police broke into her home and shot her, her eleven year old was there, and while she lay there on her floor bleeding they continued to shout at her asking her where her eldest son was. She was paralyzed from the waist down for the rest of her life.

MARIE I remember.

DAIRE   He didn't even live there.

Pigs. And they reported it as the 'Race Riots', but it wasn't that. It was rioting against authority.

MARIE   What made you come back?

DAIRE   Ah, this is my home. The best time of my life.

Our formative space isn't it. All my best memories live here. Couldn't be away from them for long. I seriously miss them. Seriously miss them. And I've come nowhere near repeating it since.

Honestly. If I could turn the clock back...

MARIE   Do you see any of them still? From your house?

DAIRE   Oh yeah. Not as much now, you know how it goes. We've become fragmented.

As things do.

I've done some stuff with the Pansies,

Casper believe it or not used to help me with My pansies, these ones—I've got a limp thumb not a green one—

He's with Philip now you know.

MARIE   I know.

DAIRE   And have you seen what they sell in WHSmiths nowadays?

Filth!

MARIE *laughs.*

DAIRE   They'll let anything in now.

Should be burned to the ground, the lot of them.

MARIE *hugs* DAIRE *and stubs out her fag.*

MARIE   I'll see you later my love.
Worlds to change, walls to paint.

DAIRE *slowly finishes their fag.*

CHAUCER/CLIFFORD   He built a garden walled about with stone;
So fair a garden do I know of none.
Which was beneath the laurel always green.
(The Merchant's Tale)

MILTON/JACK   The world was all before them, where to choose;
Their place of rest, and Providence their guide;
They, hand in hand, with wandering steps and slow,
Through Eden took their solitary way. *(Paradise Lost)*

SPENSER/CASPER   In heavenly mercies hast thou not a part?
Why shouldst thou then despeire, that chosen art?
Where justice growes, there grows eke greater grace.
(The Faerie Queene)

SHAKESPEARE/ATOM   I know a bank whereon the wild thyme blows,
Where oxlips and the nodding violet grows.
(A Midsummer Night's Dream)

End of play.

Polari Press

Taking our name from the secret slang Polari, we are an independent publishing house that seeks out hidden voices and helps them be heard.

Although Polari was spoken almost exclusively by gay and bisexual men, the nature of clandestine meetings of the mid-1900s, when homosexuality was still criminalised, brought together people from all walks of life who all had an influence on the language.

Cockney, Romany, and Italian languages mixed with the colloquialisms of thespians, circus performers, wrestlers, sailors, and wider criminal communities to create a slang to express their sexuality secretly and safely.

Inspired by these origins, we publish queer voices as well as other marginalised groups, to share our perspectives with each other and help build a collaborative platform for all of us.

polari.com

Polari Plays

We are creating an active archive for queer-authored play scripts and performance.

For a complete listing of Polari Plays titles, visit:
polari.press/plays

Follow us on social media:
@PolariPress